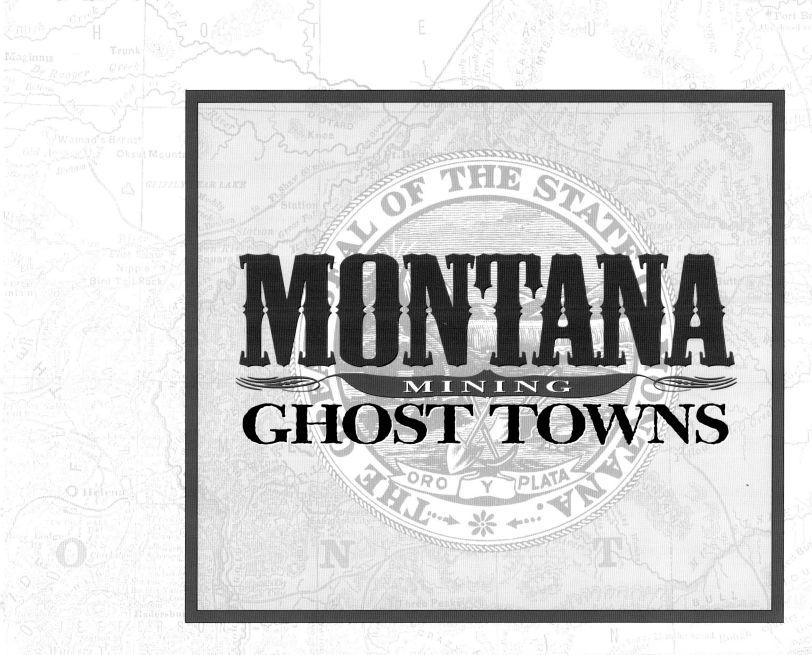

MONTANA
MINING
GHOST TOWNS

BY BARBARA FIFER

PHOTOGRAPHY BY LARRY & VIVIAN ROLAND

FARCOUNTRY
PRESS

ACKNOWLEDGMENTS

Thanks to the following individuals who helped us locate places that we visited and photographed, or allowed us to enter private property for our work: Kay Strombo, Superior; Deb Davis Quitt, Seeley Lake; Steve Jackson, Midasburg; Lloyd Harkins, Silver Star; George Byrd, Maxville; Carol Guthrie, Huson; Dale Herbort, Montana Department of Environmental Quality; the late Herb McKenzie, Missoula; Ben & Carla Andrus, Glendale; Don Beck, Garrison; William Fairhurst, Three Forks; Bob & Jenny Sitz, Harrison; Montana Territorial Land Company, Ennis; Stan Cohen, Missoula; Bill Walker Realty, Helena; Lenny Conners, Princeton.

ISBN: 1-56037-195-1

© 2002 Farcountry Press

Photography © Larry and Vivian Roland

Front cover: Granite around 1890. MONTANA HISTORICAL SOCIETY
Back cover: Lion City.

Our bookstore appears online at
www.montanamagazine.com

Created, designed and published in the USA. Printed in Korea.

TABLE OF CONTENTS

*Hard-rock miners ready to set off charges
that will dig still deeper underground.*
MONTANA HISTORICAL SOCIETY

WARNING:

Do not enter mine tunnels or shafts, and do not walk or climb on shaft covers, head-frames, or ladders associated with them. Cave-ins were common—often fatal—occurrences when mines were being worked, and are even more likely after several decades of neglect. Dry rot may have weakened the timbers, no matter how stout they appear.

Keep a safe distance from the mouths of open shafts. Some have fences and warning signs, but many do not. Even fences are no guarantee, though: The edges of these holes continue to crumble and fall in, sometimes leaving the ground outside the enclosure unsafe.

Various noxious gasses may accumulate in mines—they aren't visible, but they can kill; that's why miners often kept caged canaries underground—early versions of today's sophisticated atmosphere monitors.

This book's purpose is to preserve images of fragile ghost town structures (some of which have disappeared even since our photographs were made). Visiting ghost towns—whether on public land or, with permission, on private land—must be done with great respect and by stepping lightly on the land: take only pictures, leave only footprints.

FOREWORD

I've always been a dreamer. The books I read in my younger years fed my imagination with tales of mountain men, cowboys, buffalo hunters, the Pony Express, and…miners. Fantasies of lost treasures in abandoned ghost towns held me in particular suspense.

So, when Vivian and I moved to Montana we began to spend some of our spare time visiting the better-known mining communities in our area, bringing home photographs as our treasures. We had collected quite a few when it occurred to us that it had been over two decades since a publication of Montana's historic mining communities had been released.

Well, you know, it was a crazy idea: other people do this sort of thing, but us? We consulted a professional, who assured us that the opportunity appeared to be real, and then we began our project.

I had once said to Vivian that anybody who tried to compile photos of every former and abandoned mining town in Montana would have to be crazy, because there are simply so many. As we began the task, I asked her whether she remembered my earlier statement. "I sure do," she answered, "and you're right."

We drove thousands of miles over primary and secondary roads in Montana, as well as some that had signs beside them reading, "Primitive Road—Not Maintained for Public Use," which turned out to be the truth! Sometimes, we photographed several widely separated sites on a single day, exposing numerous rolls of film between sunrise and sunset. We followed tips and directions given to us by many helpful citizens, and pored over maps and books, attempting to track down every significant remnant of once-busy "boom" towns. Especially poignant were the evidences of family life at each of the places—a child's sled, or flowers planted long ago by a now-unknown woman.

It is doubtful whether we can ever absolutely "finish" the job—mining communities are disappearing faster now, and those who remember them are mostly gone. Those of you who also explore these places may find us, however, looking for just one more "lost" city or mine. For those who cannot go in person, we have tried to share our dream through the images you will find within the following pages. Enjoy!

Larry and Vivian Roland

It's been great fun following in the Rolands' footsteps to look for stories and background information on the Montana ghost towns they've visited (so far, that is). And, learning how much our hopeful settlements, from wild and wooly to dry and sobersided, shared with all of 19th century America.

Residents "boosted" each one as the next great city, and woe to those "croakers" who didn't jump on the bandwagon. Yet, let the rumor fly that a richer strike had appeared elsewhere, and boasts were forgotten as soon as horses were loaded to "rush" to the "new El Dorado." These men and women were willing to live in primitive conditions for their shots at fortune, but at once established or embraced finer things they'd left behind; a "professor" who came to town to teach dancing was well patronized, members of secret lodges sought out their fellows and organized, women who had to labor long and hard to make their livings (in the home or outside it) could window-shop at the milliner's or the confectioner's.

Newspapers were founded in the smallest bergs, boosting both towns and political parties; editors could freely refer to Shakespeare, Greek mythology, and the Old Testament, because even those who had to hear the news read aloud knew those sources. Residents would pull together in crises such as frequent fires and ghastly accidents, but individual ethnic groups held prejudices about each other. Then again, most of those with European heritage united in their prejudices about the red, yellow, and black people among them. The newspaper editor who could invoke the classics might also, in the very same issue, feel comfortable in offering his readers snide humor aimed at the outsiders or the displaced.

In the early days, individuals and small groups could placer alone and realize good profit on minimal investment, but those days soon passed and the available gold was buried deep in rock. While the nation industrialized, so did Montana mining, and free-roaming prospectors changed into miners working their shifts, the profit going to investors rather than locators.

Barbara Fifer

GARNET MOUNTAINS

GOLD CREEK
PIONEER CITY
WALL
BEARTOWN
COPPER CLIFF
COLOMA
GARNET
REYNOLDS CITY
SPRINGTOWN
YREKA
GARNET

Gold Creek is where it all began for Montana's mining rushes, in 1852. Soon miners were arriving from the West—not having found their fortunes in California—as well as the East. Hopeful little burgs sprang up around the area, but their loose gold didn't last long, and their hard rock mines were not the richest ones the state would see.

Above: The mail stagecoach stops in front of Judson's Store in Garnet, 1899.
MONTANA HISTORICAL SOCIETY

Below: Burned dredge at Pioneer near Gold Creek.

In a letter from Deer Lodge City:

…your people of Madison County pay little attention to the new gold mines of this region, for of the immense number of stampeders now en route to the rich diggings at BIG BEAR AND ELK CREEK, very few are from your vicinity, and the Blackfooters and Helenaites are in great glee at having the field all to themselves.

(Virginia City)
Montana Post
March 17, 1866

Gold Creek

Gold Creek was the Montana stream that first "showed colors," as prospectors called it, in 1852. Francois Finlay, a Métis (of mixed French Canadian and Indian blood) better known as Benetsee, had rushed to California when that state's first gold finds on the American River were news. After his adventure,

Benetsee was trapping for the Hudson's Bay Company east of the Continental Divide in Idaho Territory when he noticed signs he'd learned to read in California, and began dipping a pan into a creek that flowed north into the Clark Fork River.

Fully five years later, in the autumn, three prospectors also returning from California were in Utah when they heard

5

about Benetsee's find from a group, including one Robert Hereford, who had checked out the creek and didn't find enough colors to suit them. The next spring, brothers James and Granville Stuart, and Reece Anderson, located what they called Benetsee's Creek where, Granville wrote, "We found gold everywhere, in some instances as high as ten cents to the pan, but, having nothing to eat save what our rifles furnished, and no tools to work with (Salt Lake City, nearly six hundred miles distant, being the nearest point at which they could be obtained),

and as the accursed Blackfeet Indians were continually stealing our horses, we soon quit prospecting… without having found anything very rich…"

Still, the word spread, and soon about thirty men hunkered down at Gold Creek (the camp's population would max out at about forty-five). That August of 1857, three men—Arnett, Jernigan, and Spillman—arrived and opened a primitive gambling house, easily winning recently-panned gold for four glorious days. Then along came two bounty hunters to arrest the trio for horse theft. Arnett pulled a gun and was himself fatally shot, falling

with a revolver in one hand and playing cards in the other. They say the men buried him exactly that way.

The other two surrendered peaceably, were tried by a miners' court (assemblage of the whole camp), and promptly hanged. It was Montana's first vigilante justice.

Buying the needed gear from other rushers passing through from Fort Benton to new Idaho discoveries in 1862, Granville and company set up the first good sluices in future Montana. But that was the year of the fabulous Grasshopper Creek finds that created Bannack and attracted most miners away from Gold

Creek. Even the Stuart brothers headed over there for a while, before returning temporarily and then joining the Alder Gulch rush. Some miners continued collecting Gold Creek's free gold through the 1870s.

Gold Creek attracted some miners again from 1905 to 1910, and in 1930–1931, but mostly it is known simply as the place where Montana mining began.

It is also where the Northern Pacific Railroad completed its line between Minneapolis and Seattle in 1883, and the appropriately golden "last" spike in the rails was driven.

Pioneer City, Wall City

Southwest of Gold Creek, the Pioneer Mining District was organized in 1867 to include Pioneer Creek, Pioneer Gulch, and tributary gulches. Hydraulicking was the way to obtain the harder-to-retrieve gold, but the creeks tended to dry out during the short summer seasons when men gathered the gold dust that would support them through the long winter.

Stock rancher Conrad Kohrs built a sixteen-mile flume to bring in water

Nick Butler was shot in the arm at Beartown, by a man who was trying to shoot a bar-keeper....Some claims in Beargulch pay eighteen dollars per day to the man. One bar yields eight hundred to one thousand dollars per day.

(Virginia City) *Montana Post*, Sept. 22, 1866

A Beartown correspondent let neighbors know how the new camp was doing.

Among the centers of population [in Bear, Elk, and Deep gulches], Bear Town is the chief one at present....Several stores and saloons are running and doing a fair business for this season of the year. There are 5 lawyers, and I am told that all of them manage to live....I infer that this people are litigious, and have the wherewithal to grease the machinery, which else will hardly run.

(Virginia City) *Montana Post*, March 9, 1867

FROM BEARTOWN

...The last shooting affray was to have occurred between a couple of the sporting fraternity, respectively known as "Smithy" and "Collins," and that fruitful source of all the woes that man is heir to,—a woman—was the *causi belli*....On the evening of the 19th...Smithy made his appearance at the door of the club-room,...brandishing a dragoon [large hand gun] in one hand and a huge knife in the other, and ordered "that fellow Collins to come out here," adding several assertions about "chawing up," and "making mince meat," etc. They had, however, taken such extreme care to have the matter made public, that the authorities gobbled up the would be duelists, much to the satisfaction of all parties, especially the principals....

(Virginia City) *Montana Post*, Sept. 7, 1867

[After Reynolds City sprang up in 1866:] Another town, containing a number of fine buildings, was built four miles below, which the sanguine christened Yreka, really believing they had "found it"—the place they had been looking for. One year after, Yreka was deserted—the doors, windows, lumber and other valuables carted away...

(Deer Lodge) *Weekly Independent*, April 24, 1868

In February 1863, the population at Yrcka "and surroundings" was 100 people, so they deserved their own post office, the *Helena Independent* opined.

BEARTOWN.—…Some thirty men are now working and taking out money in the vicinity…About ten companys are at work on the lower gulch taking out pay dirt. Snow is two feet deep in town and about four feet at the source of the streams.…

(Deer Lodge) *Weekly Independent* , Feb. 10, 1872

In raw new communities that were both built with and heated by wood, fire was a constant—and frequently realized—threat.

FIRE AT REYNOLDS CITY—HALF THE TOWN BURNED.—The most destructive conflagration which has ever occur[r]ed in the Territory, took place at Reynolds City on the 18th inst., at fifteen minutes past three o'clock a.m. The fire broke out in Sam Ritchie's butcher shop on Main street, in the very center of town. At the time of its discovery the roof of the building was on fire and the flames spread almost instantaneously to the log buildings on each side—to the building of Boswell & Jones, dealers in general merchandise, on the one side, and on the other to the saloon of Johnny Gordon, the roof of the three buildings being on fire at the same time. The flames then spread to a building being occupied by some German shoemaker. It then consumed some eight or ten buildings that were unoccupied on the other side of the street.…

(Virginia City) *Montana Post*, Aug. 17, 1867

[An unknown person] amused himself, the other night, by profusely sprinkling one of the hurdy-gurdy floors with snuff, or cayenne pepper, or both. The girls stamped, and the boys stampeded: stamping and snuffing, sneezing and swearing, were momentarily the order.

(Virginia City) *Montana Post*, Nov. 28, 1865

from Rock Creek in 1875, and hydraulic mining reigned in Pioneer Gulch for a few years. By the late 1870s, an estimated $20 million of gold had been mined here—about $333.3 billion in today's money.

About a thousand people lived in the area, with Pioneer City their main town and service center. They included Tim Lee, who supervised 800 Chinese miners sifting through tailings and retrieving gold until the tailings yielded no more. Other Chinese miners reworked tailings in various parts of the district.

An English company began dredging in this area in the 1890s, but long-time miners didn't like it, and Kohrs led a group who cut off their supplies, water, and timber. The corporation answered with a lawsuit, which continued all the way to 1927. It finally ended when a Butte miner, Pat Wall, bought the English firm's holdings and also those of Kohrs, including water rights and the Pioneer City townsite. He set up significant dredging and hydraulicking operations. Most of the district's gold had been found before 1900, but Wall mined nearly $1.4 million worth between 1933 and 1939.

Above and left: Pioneer City.

Facing page, top left: At Beartown, these are the remains of a powder house that later was used as a jail.

Facing page, top right: Water still surges seasonally through a Beartown mill race.

Facing page, bottom left: North of Bearmouth was this water-powered arrastra, with a 20-foot-diameter horizontal water wheel.

MONTANA HISTORICAL SOCIETY

Facing page, bottom right: Copper Cliff storefront.

Beartown

Placer-gold prospectors struck gold in 1865 where Bear Creek flows into the Clark Fork River, and christened the area Bearmouth, the name it holds today. In three years, the camp of Beartown began to grow, six miles up Bear Creek, offering saloons and gambling houses, several stores, and a blacksmith shop.

Water had to be brought in by flumes, including one that flowed through a mountainside tunnel. Thirty-five miners joined to build a million-dollar water tank in 1896 to continue working their placer claims. An estimated $7 million in placer gold came out of here by 1917. The free gold deposits were narrow, but the richest ones produced $1,200 to the foot. As the placer yield began to lessen, miners began digging underground. By the early 1880s, arrastras processed gold and silver ore from several small mines. Concentrated ore then was hauled by wagon down to the Northern Pacific Railroad at Bearmouth for shipment to smelters in East Helena or Butte. Beartown was so settled that it

opened a school in 1881.

Water had carried the area's placer gold down into Bear Gulch from the lode deposits at Garnet, which was at Bear Creek's headwaters.

Copper Cliff Mine, Leonard Mine

The Copper Cliff Mining District, named for a 150-foot-high quartz cliff, produced ore of copper laced with small amounts of gold and silver, beginning in 1891. Through 1960 it produced a little

NEW DITCH.—A new ditch is now being surveyed for the purpose of increasing the supply of water at Pioneer City and vicinity....This will open up a large extent of ground believed to be rich.

(Deer Lodge)
Weekly Independent
Nov. 7, 1868

CHINESE MINERS—WITH RESTRICTIONS

Chinese people who came to the United States during the last half of the 19th century built railroads, roads, and buildings, mined, operated small businesses, and lived under extensive legal restrictions. While many came temporarily and returned home with their savings, thousands stayed and contributed to an America that had been reluctant to welcome them.

The U.S. Census of 1870 counted nearly 2,000 Chinese residents in Montana, which meant they lived in the new mining camps in the state's southwest. By Montana Territory law, Chinese and blacks were not allowed to marry or live with whites. "Chinatown" districts already had developed in Alder and Last Chance gulches by local edict. Virginia City made a point of allowing Chinese men to open certain businesses in the main business district—those that were useful to the town and didn't compete with white-owned concerns.

Wallace Street business, Virginia City.
MONTANA HISTORICAL SOCIETY

The Chinese were allowed to run laundries, fresh-produce shops, and restaurants. In Last Chance Gulch's early years, Chinese-owned truck gardens were the main local source of vegetables. As for laundries, the territorial legislature added financial injury to insult with a special annual license fee of $40, raised to $60 and then to $80, for males who "engaged" in the business. In today's dollars, those licenses cost from $500 to $888 per year.

In 1872, the territorial legislature banned all aliens from owning or profiting from mines. After territorial Chief Justice Decius Wade shot down the law by saying that federal law overrode it, territorial courts merely interpreted federal laws to create the same result. Even as delegates sat down in 1889 to write the first statehood constitution, some tried to include restrictions on Chinese residents in this basic document.

The solution to the mining ban was that Chinese miners leased rights to mining sites from the white owners who considered them worked out. Since the impatient owners were giving up early and looking for the next easy pickings, careful work by anyone would uncover more gold or silver. The Chinese, taking advantage of limited opportunity, got a reputation for an uncanny ability to wring gold from the ground. In truth, they moved and washed tons of gravel by hand, and diligent efforts paid off for all miners. At site after site around Montana, Chinese miners moved in when whites moved on and allowed them a try.

over a quarter million pounds of copper, 259 ounces of gold, and 567 ounces of silver. Its creeks flow north as tributaries of the Blackfoot River, and its mine adits enter the ground at about 5,000 feet in elevation.

The Copper Cliff and the Leonard were the two most important mines in the district. Although the Copper Cliff had four tunnels by 1919 when its third owner, Potomac Copper Company, took over, the ore cost more to mine than it was worth. The Leonard, started in 1913, also was of little value, but during World War II, Ole Dahl relocat-

ed the mine, renamed it the Blue Bell, and shipped copper, silver, and lead ore worth less than $1,200.

Coloma, Reynolds City, Springtown, Yreka

Placer gold discoveries in the Coloma Mining District date from 1865, when a major rush occurred and the names Bivins Gulch and Elk Creek were on every prospector's tongue. The rush gave birth to the towns of

Facing page, top: Looking out of the Leonard Mine adit at Copper Cliff.

Facing page, bottom: Coloma's main street.

Coloma, Reynolds City, Springtown, and Yreka, each of which expected a bright and lengthy future. Weather permitting, daily stagecoach service soon connected Coloma with Bearmouth—a rugged ride through the Garnet Mountains. Four thousand miners lived and worked between the two points by the 1880s. A ten-stamp and a twenty-stamp mill at Coloma crushed their ore before it was carted out to Montana smelters. But no one got rich placering in the district, which is estimated to have produced no more than $100,000 in free gold.

Late in the 1890s, lode veins were discovered near the town of Coloma, and the town tottered on into the twentieth century producing low-value ore. Even the largest mines, the Mammoth (opened 1896) and the Comet (opened about 1905), were not profitable for their investors. The Mammoth offered up gold, silver, lead, and zinc, and the Comet a small amount of gold.

The strikes at Reynolds City, Springtown, and Yreka had short lives before they played out. Not many people gathered at each settlement, and most were gone after two seasons.

Garnet

Historian John Ellingsen wrote: "Garnet did not produce the first gold [in Montana], the last gold, the most gold, or the biggest nuggets." But it did survive, and today has its own Garnet Preservation Society, which raises money and works to stabilize and reconstruct buildings there.

Placer gold strikes in the northern part of the Garnet Range began in 1865, but not until the 1890s was the town of Garnet founded. It's fondly called

Top left: This Coloma cabin had a storm entrance.

Top right: Garnet, with Kelly's Saloon at center, Frank Davey's store to the right, and the J. K. Wells Hotel beyond. Across from them is Ole Dahl's house.

Right: Home away from home, for some of the boys.

Montana made its second try for statehood in 1884, after twenty years as a territory. Residents thought statehood was a sure thing, but the national political balance would keep Montana from full membership in the Union for five more years. However, some residents obviously weren't impressed with the effort:

The framers of the [state] constitution closed their labors by singing the "Star Spangled Banner." This was probably the hardest work they have done during the session.

(Maiden)
Mineral Argus
Feb. 21, 1884

Left: J.K. Wells Hotel in Garnet.

Below left: Davey's Store, Garnet (foreground), and Kelly's Saloon.

Below: One of Garnet's caved-in mine tunnels.

Mr. Errick [in Beartown] lost half a dozen chickens the other evening, supposed to have been confiscated for culinary purposes by parties whose consciences are not so tender as the said chickens proved to be when dished up....

(Deer Lodge) *Weekly Independent* Feb. 10, 1872

"Montana's last gold-rush camp," but lode mining rather than placering in the streams is what brought miners here.

Dr. Peter Mussigbrod, the contractor who had built the Territorial Prison and the "mental asylum" at Warm Springs, put in a ten-stamp mill at the site, and it opened in 1895 under the management of A. H. Mitchell. The mill processed ore from the doctor's ten claims, and also for ten or so others. The town that bloomed around the mill was first called Mitchell in the manager's honor; the good doctor's name was spelled in various ways, including a reference to his self-named mine as the intriguing "Music Bread." When Mitchell obtained a post office in 1897, it served 100 addressees in town (and about a thousand area miners). The town's name was changed to Garnet the same year.

The growing center offered certain amenities: besides thirteen saloons and at least one brothel, there were one each of candy shop, butcher, assay office, doctor, and school, two laundries and barber shops, three livery stables, four hotels, and several mining-company boarding houses. Garnet was on the daily stage route to Bearmouth at the Northern Pacific Railroad.

Back in 1873, Samuel I. Ritchey (also recorded as Ritchie and Richey) had struck gold right outside Garnet in a mine he named the Nancy Hanks after the mother of Abraham Lincoln. Now, in 1896, he found the richest vein off to the side of the original shaft. He put two shifts of twelve men to work, twenty-four hours a day, following the vein, and also hired twenty miners to work the profitable Shamrock Mine that he had located in 1867. The Nancy Hanks produced well for three years, then the vein began to thin out, and the mine was closed in 1916, six years after Ritchey had ended connections to it. The mine had produced at least $300,000, although the records are incomplete and some people have pegged its yield to $10 million.

The turn of the 20th century was Garnet's high tide. By 1905, lodes were fading away and miners losing their jobs; its population had dropped to 200. Six years later a fire burned down a building on one side of Main Street, jumped the street and took out all but one of the businesses on the other side.

The short flurry of prospecting in the mid-1930s brought people back into Garnet, but by 1942 the town was considered abandoned—except for one resident, owner of Davey's Store. When told by the Internal Revenue Service to sign a tax form before a witness, Frank Davey stood before a mirror, signed, and witnessed himself, then attached a note explaining that he was the sole resident of an abandoned gold camp.

GRASSHOPPER CREEK

Despite its isolated location in rugged country, Bannack was rich in placer gold—and, it seems, most everything else that would later find its way into the motion pictures: a sheriff so crooked that he actually led the outlaws, proper New England lawyers who set the rough settlement on its path to statehood, Vigilantes, honorable members of the Masonic brotherhood, a schoolmarm named Miss Darling, hard-working and hard-playing miners, and the low-life men and women who preyed upon them.

Bannack

Wild and wooly Bannack holds a whole fistful of firsts for Montana, as it should, since the rush here created Montana Territory.

The first recorded white people to visit Grasshopper Creek were a part of the Lewis and Clark Expedition, led through here by Captain William Clark in July 1806. They weren't prospecting for gold—although one of their charges from President Thomas Jefferson was to record signs of mineral wealth they noticed—they were heading home in the twenty-sixth month of their twenty-eight-month trek. Clark named the trickle "Willard's Creek" for Private Alexander Willard of the company, but like most of the names bestowed by the Corps of

Above: Bannack during its 1860s heyday.
MONTANA HISTORICAL SOCIETY

Below: Bannack's Meade Hotel.

A Bannack correspondent wanted to let other miners know that Grasshopper Creek's riches hadn't played out yet:

Quite a number of Bannackites have…returned from the new mines, to make a "raise" at Bannack…frequently when a new gulch is struck…there are not less than five hundred people to a claim. Let them come to Bannack—there is no richer gulch in the Territory than this, and the untold millions of the very best kind of gold dust still slumbers [*sic*] beneath [G]rasshopper.

(Virginia City)
Montana Post
July 21, 1866

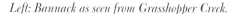

Left: Bannack as seen from Grasshopper Creek.

Below left: Ore cars at Bannack; the Jackson House beyond belonged to the Goodrich Hotel owners, and also housed a post office.

Below right: Pete Daly's stage station— "Robbers' Roost"—in the 1890s.

MONTANA HISTORICAL SOCIETY

Sunday was a "lively day" according to the phraseology of the country. There was one display of the "manly" art, and some bloody faces, and a one-horse race. A horse was won and lost....

letter from Bannack to the (Virginia City) *Montana Post* July 21, 1866

Discovery, this one didn't stick.

The excited Coloradans John White and William Eades who knew they'd struck it rich here in July 1862 didn't know about Clark's naming, but they knew that the name Gold Creek was already taken. Those finds were what had drawn them north. They settled for Grasshopper Creek, because there seemed to be as many of those in the air as there were flakes of pure gold in the pan. Soon a scrawled sign was posted: THIS WAY TO GRASSHOPER DIGGINS. Soon, too, there was a mushrooming town, styled Bannack in a misspelling of the name of the Bannock Indians who lived

in this eastern part of Idaho Territory.

Four hundred people moved in that summer, throwing up log cabins and creating dugouts for the winter ahead. They included James and Granville Stuart, who had started panning at Gold Creek four years earlier, and now brought in a herd of cattle and opened a butcher shop.

The population grew tenfold or more in the next season, although supplies had to come by ox train from the Union Pacific railhead at Corinne, Utah (leaving ruts that still are visible), and could arrive only during summer. Saloons, sporting houses, and gambling parlors sprang up to relieve miners of their dust.

A handsome fellow with the manners of a gentleman showed up, saying he'd tried his luck in California. The miners elected him sheriff, and didn't ask Henry Plummer what he'd tried his luck at.

"Road agents" (highway robbers), committed about 100 murders along with many more robberies, mostly on the road from Bannack to Virginia City. In the cold early months of 1864, Vigilantes cleaned up the area (see "The Vigilance Committee," page 23).

Community leaders—many of whom were also Vigilantes—petitioned to be separated from Idaho Territory, and in May 1864, Montana Territory was creat-

ed with Bannack as its capital. The Vigilantes could stop riding by night now that the seat of law and order was here rather than days away.

Now the problem became big gold strikes elsewhere in Montana Territory. Miners rushed off for Last Chance Gulch (future Helena) and to Alder Gulch, where Virginia City was building. In December 1864, the first territorial legislature saw fit to move the capital to Virginia City.

Bannack's placer gold was getting scarcer, and had been since the year before, when the Stuart brothers had closed their butcher shop and headed back to Gold Creek.

But only the easy gold was gone, some $3 million worth of it between 1862 and 1876. Hydraulic and lode mining, followed by dredging, would continue to extract the riches, but to a lesser degree. James Fergus had located and worked the Dakota Claim at Bannack in November 1862, which held Montana's first quartz gold lode. A blacksmith promptly put together the area's first stamp mill from spare parts of freight wagons.

A few other lodes were worked through the 1870s, but they required much more effort than did placering. Profits went to the owners, or the investors (called "capitalists" in newspapers of the time); actual miners merely earned salaries.

A dishonest miner might steal small chunks of high-grade ore, stashing it in a pocket or the lunch bucket each man always carried. The practice soon was called "high grading," a slang term still in use in Montana to mean appropriating someone else's property or else taking the easy pickings.

By the 1890s, fifty or so miners were employed in a handful of Bannack lode mines by Gold Leaf Mining Company, Ltd., of Great Britain. The company built a larger mill and put electric power into the mines, but the veins were running out.

Top left: The first Territorial Legislature met here at Bannack, 1863.
MONTANA HISTORICAL SOCIETY

Top right: Montana Territory's first "governor's mansion," home to Sidney Edgerton in 1863, as it looked in 1908.
MONTANA HISTORICAL SOCIETY

Right: Bannack's Methodist Church, at right, was founded in 1870 by pioneering missionary W.W. "Brother Van" Van Orsdel. The Fielding L. Graves residence stands at left.

Angling.—The disciples of Isaac Walton [In 1653, Isaak Walton wrote on the joys of fishing.] are having rare sport at the present time in this vicinity. The members of the finny tribe have left the river and ascended the small streams in great numbers. A string of a dozen is not more than average for two hours' fishing in any of the streams in this valley at present. The denizens of the metropolis [Helena] should shake off the dust of the city and come over here and spend a week, if they would enjoy life.

(Deer Lodge)
Weekly Independent
May 29, 1869

Pete Daly's stage stop should be named "Ten-Dog Station" for its "multitude of canine warders," a Deer Lodge City correspondent wrote to the *Montana Post* in December 1865.

Bannack's last round of innovation came in 1895, and was the first successful gold dredging in the United States. The *Fielding L. Graves*'s connected buckets, powered by an electrical generator on shore, could chew through 2,000 cubic yards of Grasshopper Creek gravel a day. Two steam-powered dredges, less economical and efficient, soon joined it (a fourth sank upon launch and a fifth was put into nearby Spring Gulch), but by 1902 the gold in commercial quantities was gone. C. W. Stallings made a living beginning in 1918 with the Hendricks Lode mine, employing ten miners, reporting in 1940 that the total production had been about $40,000.

The town's frame and log buildings were cannibalized and vandalized over the years, and just plain beat down by the weather. In 1953, Stallings was the townsite's last resident; he bought Bannack from a bankrupt mining company for $1,400, and sold it at a loss the next year to citizen groups organized to protect the old capital. That was the first step in creating Bannack State Park, which was named a national historic landmark on its hundredth birthday in 1962. Buildings have been stabilized, and on the third weekend of July each year, Bannack comes back to life with reenactors, craft demonstrations, and maybe a shooting or hanging or two.

Above left: Summer's "Bannack Days" bring visitors to Bannack State Park for demonstrations, food, and reenactments.

Above right: Skinner's Saloon was one of the places where road agents planning to schedule robberies eavesdropped on miners' travel plans.

Below left: Montana's first school house was the downstairs of the building at right, taught by Gov. Edgerton's niece Lucia Darling. The Masonic Hall filled the second story.

Below right: Some Bannack graves had their own enclosures.

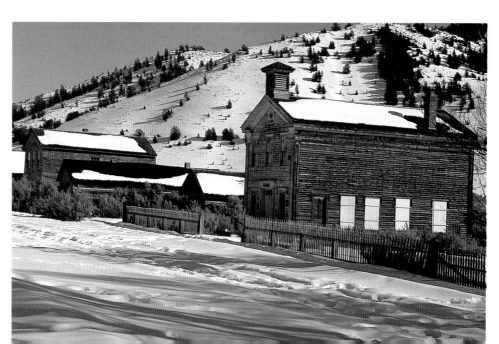

ALDER GULCH

In no time at all after miners found placer gold at Virginia City, strikes all along Alder Gulch created a string of raw mining camps that residents proudly claimed as the "fourteen-mile city." Today, Virginia City is half living town and half preserved ghost town, Nevada City has been recreated, and Alder Gulch is Montana's best place for returning to the frontier past and imagining the struggle between those who wanted to import Civilization and those who'd come here to escape from it.

Above: Virginia City, 1866, with rich Alder Gulch in the foreground.
MONTANA HISTORICAL SOCIETY

Below: Madison County Court House in the "living" portion of Virginia City.

The Territorial Legislature was holding its third regular session late in 1866...er, sort of:

An aperture has been cut in the stone wall which separates the El Sol Billiard Hall and the Council [Senate] Chamber, and a door now makes it easy for the members to go from one point to the other....The objects of this work of internal improvement can be imagined better than they can be described.

(Virginia City)
Montana Post
Dec. 8, 1866

Virginia City

Bannack's placers had just begun a downturn when Bill Fairweather, Henry F. Edgar, and four other prospectors made a failed attempt to see what the Yellowstone River might hold. Crow Indians gave them the idea of heading back west, and kept most of their baggage in the process. The miners were closer to Bannack than Crow Country when they decided to dip a pan into a little creek late one May afternoon.

Fairweather and Edgar kept watch for Indians during the day while the others panned. The return was all right but not spectacular. When Fairweather crossed the creek to tie up their horses that evening, though, he saw rich-looking exposed rock. He and Edgar dug and

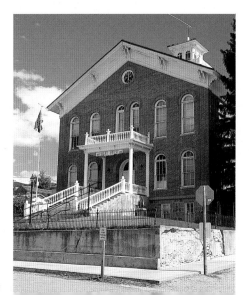

In mining camps, composed of logs and wood-frame buildings, and in those days heated by wood or coal stoves, structure fires were a constant danger. Frigid winter weather only increased the danger, but after a fire was successfully fought, there was always a moment for a little humor.

FIRE.—About ten o'clock on Thursday evening, the alarm of fire sounded in our streets and brought from their cosy firesides to their doors in a hurry, whole hosts of startled denizens peeping out like so many prairire [*sic*] dogs from their mounds. The alarm was occasioned by some wood piled beside a stove in Col. [Wilbur Fisk] Sanders' office…The fire communicated to the floor, and as a lawyer['s] office is about the dryest [*sic*] place in christendom, it was soon in a beautiful state of combustion. Fortunately the smoke…attracted attention…and the fire [was] extinguished before any very considerable damage was done.

(Virginia City)
Montana Post
Jan. 11, 1868

washed gravel for a while, delighted with what they saw. The next day all six men worked the gulch, coming up with $180 worth of gold—in 1863 dollars.

With no supplies, they had to return to Bannack. Each man carefully staked out two claims, even though they hoped to keep the find secret. It was good they marked their choices, because 200 men returned with them on June 6. In a year, the gulch had 10,000 residents. Claims ran up Alder Gulch and intersecting gulches, and into the surrounding mountains. Townsites were platted north along Alder Creek, beginning with Virginia

City at the discovery site, then on through Nevada City, Adobetown, and Laurin, among others.

The placer gold flowed generously for five years, totalling an estimated $30 to $40 million. Placering continued until 1886 while Chinese miners profitably reworked tailings left by earlier miners, and those years added another $10 million to the district's placer take.

Life in Alder Gulch was violent. Even placer mining was dangerous, and as the first drifts were dug into the ground, they began causing injuries and fatalities. Regular shootings erupted over mining

claims and lovers' claims and political and lesser disagreements. Bannack's crooked sheriff, Henry Plummer, forced Virginia City's first sheriff to let him claim jurisdiction over both towns—until his own criminal acts were discovered. The Vigilantes created some order, then they lowered the bar too far on what was a hanging offense, and law-abiding residents as well as crooks were glad to see them disband. Runaway horses—under saddle, pulling carriages or, worse, heavy freight wagons—were a constant danger on the streets, and fire easily could have taken down the whole crowded frame

Top left: Four road agents were hanged by the Vigilantes here, while the building was under construction.

Above: Henry F. Edgar posed on a return visit to Alder Gulch in 1899.
MONTANA HISTORICAL SOCIETY

Left: The Smith and Boyd Saloon in 1900; it later was known as the Bale of Hay Saloon.
MONTANA HISTORICAL SOCIETY

Facing page, top: For the finest duds in Virginia City, check out this Bovey acquisition.

Bottom: Quenching Virginia City's thirst.

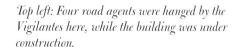

and log town of the earliest days.

The Civil War was still in progress during 1863, and it so happened that about half the miners were Union and half were Confederate. The latter tried to name the first town Varina City for Mrs. Jefferson Davis, wife of the Confederacy's president, but a pro-Union judge changed it to Virginia for a state split in its sympathies. One of the murderers hanged by the Vigilantes used his opportunity for last words to shout, "Every man for his principles. Hurrah for Jeff Davis!" When news of President Abraham Lincoln's assassination arrived two weeks after his death and less than a year after he signed the bill creating Montana Territory, half the town celebrated with gunshots while the other half mourned.

Despite the surrounding roughness, many Virginia City residents worked to establish "civilization" here, and an informal lending library was among their first creations. A Jesuit, the Rev. Joseph Giorda, first celebrated mass here in a dirt-floored log cabin in the fall of 1863 and the first resident Catholic priest arrived in 1869. Protestants organized to build a nondenominational church, the Union Church, in 1864; Methodists built their

Bare-knuckle boxing matches—and the betting that accompanied them—were frequent entertainments. Obviously, the participants took their reputations seriously. Thus, this advertisement appeared in the November 4, 1864, issue of Virginia City's *Montana Post*:

A CHALLENGE

Having heard that Tom. [*sic*] Foster is dissatisfied with the result of his fight with me, and thinks he would have a better show in Bannack, I do hereby challenge him to fight me a fair stand up fight anywhere within 100 miles of this city [for a purse of "any amount over $1,000"]. **Put up or shut up. Joseph Riley**

Riley received this lukewarm review—complete with misspelled name—from the same paper the following August:

At the sparring match in Leviathan Hall, there was not much worthy of note. Joe Reilly appears a good deal steadier and more finished in his deliveries and stops.

Life in mining camps held dangers on all sides, as revealed in these stories from the Helena correspondent in the February 24, 1866, *Montana Post*:

FROZEN TO DEATH.—On the trail from Uncle Johnny's Gulch to Diamond City, an unfortunate man, whose name is unknown, was found frozen to death, a few days since....

MYSTERIOUS DISAPPEARANCE.—N. Smith, a musician, suddenly disappeared from a dance house, in Diamond City, leaving his instrument behind him. No trace can be found of the missing man. Every pit and shaft has been examined. Foul play is suspected. He had, the day before, weighed his money [in the form of gold dust] in the saloon, amounting to about one hundred and fifty dollars [about $1,666 today].

FATAL ACCIDENT.—Two men, Michael McDonnel and Thos. Kevlehan, engaged in drifting in Confederate Gulch, at a depth of forty feet, and at a distance of seventy feet from the entrance, lost their lives by the caving in of their work. Only after twenty-four hours of ceaseless and energetic labor were their lifeless bodies recovered.

ANOTHER VICTIM OF FROST.—On Sunday...the body of a man was brought into town, and recognized as Phillip Farley, of Silver Creek. The nose, one cheek and an ear were eaten off by mice, which greatly disfigured the body, and it was hard for his friends to recognize him....He had been on the Sun river stampede, and met his fate during the extremely cold and stormy weather of January.

HURDY-GURDY HOUSES

Frontier dance halls sometimes were just that, with a husband as bartender and his wife managing the women dance partners, but often they fronted houses of prostitution. Besides paying for each dance, the customers were expected to buy the women overpriced drinks between dances. ("Champagne" was $12 a bottle, $133 in today's money, and poor whiskey sold for 50¢ a shot, or $5.50.) Late in winter, though, a miner's gold dust from the last season would be running low.

A revival in hurdy-gurdyism is in progress, four ladies from Germany acting as priestesses, and the old California Exchange serving as a temple. Spiritual consolation alternates with the mystic finger-shaking rites, even as in the days of last Summer, when ye honest [miner] had plenty of cash for contributions.
(Virginia City) *Montana Post*, March 10, 1866

Only a week after that story, the same editor had a new opinion.

In Virginia City, hurdy gurdies are on the way out: We cannot see any reason for regretting this change in our programme of amusements. The theatre affords substantial gratification and innocent recreation, at much less cost. The professional dancers have, as a rule, gained little by these houses beyond a current subsistence; the proprietors have not been financially benefited to any extent...
(Virginia City) *Montana Post*, March 17, 1866

That fall, a letter signed "Subscriber" described what it was like to be a hurdy-gurdy's unwilling neighbor:

EDITOR POST:—Why don't you pitch into that infernal nuisance on Jackson street, called by some a dance house?

I live a few doors from it, and nearly every night my rest is broken by the shouts of drunken prostitutes and their partners. Sometimes the tumult lasts until morning, and it is high time that this sink of infamy is removed. Fights are always occurring and the dancers utter, hour after hour[,] the most profane and obscene remarks. Many fools throw away their money here, and we shall be obliged to support them the coming winter...
(Virginia City) *Montana Post*, Sept. 22, 1866

The women employed in the houses were not the mining camps' best citizens, as these two stories from Last Chance Gulch illustrate.

...On Thursday evening Kate Silvers, one of the nymphs of one of the free and easy dance houses, probably under the influence of bad whisky, not having the fear of the police before her eyes, committed an assault on Tom McNally, the bar keeper of the house. Quite a lively fistical set-to ensued, when she was taken in charge by the police officer, until all her fury was spent in words that would sound better coming from the tongue of the roughest of the sterner sex. The quarrel was caused by McNally trying to persuade her to take a partner for the next dance.
"Helena Notes," (Virginia City) *Montana Post*, Sept. 29, 1866

...Kate Silvers who[,] having brought from "Confederate [Gulch]," where she had been doing business this summer, the lawless manners of that bad place, drew a Derringer on the keeper of the Free Concert, Thursday night, but...probably, in consideration of her youth and beauty, was not arrested. Miss Silvers is a rather brassy one.
"Helena Notes," (Virginia City) *Montana Post*, Oct. 6, 1866

own log chapel the same year. *Montana Post* newspaper editor Thomas Dimsdale began teaching school in borrowed space in the Union Church in August 1864, and soon eighty-one pupils attended classes in a two-room log school taught by Mrs. Sarah Herndon.

Charity and holiday balls, banquets, sleigh-ride excursions, and other "jollities" helped pass the long winter. The popular fraternal orders erected lodge buildings that did double duty as public halls for dances, traveling lecturers and entertainers, and homegrown revues and musicales. Quite aware they were making histo-

Virginia City's Dance & Stuart Store was one of Granville Stuart's many enterprises.

ALDER GULCH

ry, leading citizens formed the Historical Society of Montana, direct predecessor of the Montana Historical Society that now cares for the town's historic district.

Chinese residents, an estimated 500 in Alder Gulch, were restricted to a residential district where Main Street ran into Alder Gulch. Besides homes of various degrees of prosperity, there were restaurants, saloons, and gambling parlors, but the two-story temple building was the community's social as well as religious center. In it, a separate Chinese lodge of Masons met, down the hill from their brethren in the order. Chi-

nese owners were allowed to run some businesses, primarily restaurants and laundries, on Virginia City's main street. Religious celebrations, funerals, and smaller events involving Chinese people were covered in the newspaper with snickering tone and racist vocabulary in the early years.

Virginia City won the territorial capital from Bannack in 1865 and lost it to Helena ten years later. The legislature met in rented space here just as it had at Bannack. After 1875, Virginia City settled into life as seat and central town of Madison County.

Top left: Virginia City's Chinese temple.
MONTANA HISTORICAL SOCIETY

Top right: An authentically stocked mercantile.

Above: Inside Virginia City's Chinese temple.
MONTANA HISTORICAL SOCIETY

Right: Montana territorial governor (1870–1883) Benjamin F. Potts stands at left on the balcony, outside his Executive Building office, Virginia City in 1874; at right is territorial auditor George Callaway.
MONTANA HISTORICAL SOCIETY

As a benefit for the town's "poor children"—and also an occasion for indoor fun during the long winter—Virginia City held a "calico ball." Ladies' gowns had to be made from that everyday cotton cloth, but obviously ingenuity made up for the restriction. Results left the newspaper's editor a bit breathless:

Robed in all the varied designs and artful simplicity into which plain, figured, barred or colored calico can be gored, gussetted, trimmed, braided, puffed, or the thousand and other, to us, nameless and incomprehensible methods and devices the ladies have of cutting, clipping, sewing and twisting cotton fabrics until they finally twist themselves inside of them…

(Virginia City)
Montana Post
Jan. 25, 1868

Left: Virginia City from Boot Hill.

Below: Named for one of Alder Gulch's discoverers, the Fairweather Inn today offers frontier-style lodging in Virginia City.

Above: Virginia City.

Left: The results of early hydraulic mining, shot near Virginia City in 1871. Instead of waiting for gold to wash out into creeks, miners took down hillsides with high-pressure streams of water.
MONTANA HISTORICAL SOCIETY

Facing page: The working heart of a gold dredge, Nevada City.

ON ICE.—The informal inauguration of the skating pond took place on Saturday afternoon…In stating that it was a success from the start, it is superfluous to add that a number of ladies graced the scene and gave a tone of *gallantry* to what otherwise might have been a very *boisterous* crowd…. Virginia is following closely in the wake of metropolitan cities, and the probability is that by next year,…we will have an opera house here and a summer resort on the lakes. So be it.

(Virginia City)
Montana Post
Jan. 18, 1868

But Alder Gulch hadn't yet given up all its gold, and in 1899 the Conrey Placer Mining Company put in the first of six dredges that worked the creek. When Conrey closed down in 1922, it sold off removable machinery and left the wooden platforms sitting in the water. Over twenty-four years, dredging dug up 37 million cubic yards of the gulch between Virginia City and the town of Alder, for $9 million worth of gold.

Lode mining in the surrounding mountains had begun in 1864, with arrastras to extract free milling gold from ore dug in shallow mines. These deposits lasted about ten years, with one mine alone producing $1.25 million. Quartz mining was mainly in the Summit district south of Virginia City and in Brown's Gulch. In the 1880s and 1890s, most area mines were very small ones, and the pattern repeated during the Great Depression of the 1930s. Larger mines dug into poorer and poorer ore, depending on cyanide processing to retrieve as little as 0.27 ounces of gold and 1.11 ounces of silver per ton in the 1920s.

The oldest part of Virginia City was abandoned and left to sit empty as peo-

ple moved away in the 1920s and 1930s. Right after World War II, Charles and Sue Ford Bovey began to put their energy, personal fortune, and fund-raising skills to work in preserving and restoring what is now the historic district—from entire buildings right down to goods that stock store shelves. Their son sold the property to the State of Montana in the 1990s. Virginia City never became a true ghost town, and its western side—now a state park—is very much like what it was at the beginning.

Nevada City, Laurin,
Robbers' Roost, Brandon

Two miles down Alder Gulch from Virginia City stands Nevada City, its few streets neatly gridded on a flat near the once-rich creek. But only parts of it are original on this spot, so Nevada City—for different reasons—is no more a true ghost town than half-living Virginia City. But that's been okay with non-purist visitors, and several film companies, since the early 1960s.

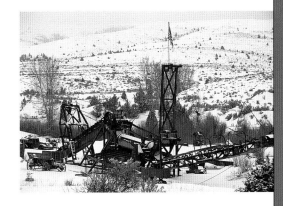

The real Nevada City began when Virginia City and the rest of the string of hastily thrown together towns began to fill Alder Gulch in 1862. Miners were proud to call the gulch's settlements a

THE VIGILANCE COMMITTEE

Vigilantes answered the first needs for frontier law enforcement in Bannack and Alder Gulch. Organized by men of various social levels, the Vigilance Committee had an oath and bylaws but kept its membership rolls secret. Members included citizens such as Wilbur Fisk Sanders, James and Granville Stuart, and Robert Hereford (who drew the Stuarts to Montana).

James Stuart, Granville's brother, died of illness in 1873.

After accusing and trying a man on the spot, the committee at once determined his punishment. Frequently they demanded only that he leave the territory.

"GONE TO HIS DEATH."—We have the rumor from a perfectly reliable source, that George Rosenbaum, who was whipped and banished from this place by the Vigilantes, during the last autumn, was hanged in Nevada [City] a day or two ago. The telegram gives no particulars, but it is presumed the Vigilantes did the good work, as we have seen no mention of his arrest or his trial in any of our exchanges [newspapers]. Rosenbaum was a notorious scoundrel, and the world is well rid of him.

(Virginia City) *Montana Post*, Feb. 2, 1867

But not everyone approved of the Vigilantes, or what happened in their name. Only a month after the above story, this was posted at Red Mountain City in Highland Mining District:
NOTICE!
We now, as a sworn band of law-abiding citizens, do hereby solemnly swear that the first man that is hung by the Vigilantes of this place, we will retaliate five for one, unless it be done in broad daylight, so that all may know what it is for. We are all well satisfied that, in times past, you did some glorious work, but the time has come when law should be enforced. Old fellow-members, the time is not like it was. We had good men with us; but, now, there is a great change. There is not a thief comes to this country but what "rings" himself into the present committee. We know you all. You must not think you can do as you please. We are American citizens, and you shall not drive [out], and hang, whom you please.

(SIGNED) FIVE FOR ONE

(Virginia City) *Montana Post*, March 2, 1867

And, three months later:
VIGILANCE COMMITTEE VS. ROWDYISM
Things in and about Red Mountain City assumed a very belligerent shape on Sunday last...It seems that the Vigilance Committee were notified that a certain individual...had been robbed the night previously by his paramour...of upwards of $1,000 in gold dust. The Vigilance Committee took the case in hand, and arrested the parties about 3 o'clock in the afternoon and marched them to a house about a quarter mile below town, where they were followed by a few of the anti kind, who demanded admission into the house...

After interrogating the woman and getting the money returned, the committee turned "the case" over to authorities. The letter recounting this incident ended with the opinion:
We think...that the Vigilance Committee of this section mean business, and that they will have peace and quiet at all hazards in the future.

(Virginia City) *Montana Post*, June 15, 1867

No one knows for sure what their mysterious motto "3-7-77" means to this day, but it still adorns the insignia of the Montana Highway Patrol.

Left: Nevada City.

Below: Most buildings seen today at Nevada City have been moved from various Montana locations. The Sedman House, seen here, is from Junction City.

"fourteen-mile city." Nevada City and Virginia City share the same mining and social history but, with a smaller initial population and no county seat of government to keep it going, Nevada City got off the train earlier.

At its peak, Nevada City was about one fifth the size of Virginia City. Its residents began drifting away by 1868, looking for another placer strike, and those who stayed happily tore down empty buildings for firewood. Nearby is the rich Brown's Gulch, which was lode-mined into the early 20th century, but its workers probably went home to

Virginia City after their shifts. By the late 1940s, only two or three buildings remained somewhat intact on the site.

In 1960, Charles Bovey needed Nevada City. He liked to collect things—big things. He had purchased buildings around the state and moved them to Great Falls, his home town. He bought coin-operated mechanical marvels from the late 1800s and early 1900s, too: player pianos, a carousel's pipe organ, a combination piano and violin that played classical motifs, a hand-cranked kinescope movie viewer, and many, many more. Beginning in 1940, many ended up in the

Above: Nevada City exhibits this simplest form of the arrastra.

Left: Wallace Street, Virginia City.

Facing page, top left: Site of the Fairview Mine, north of Virginia City.

Facing page, top right: Looking west along Nevada City's California Street.

Facing page, bottom left: Laurin's Catholic church was built in 1902.

Facing page, bottom right: Former Morrison's Mercantile, Laurin.

buildings he exhibited at his "Old Town" on the state fairgrounds in Great Falls.

Then the fair board needed room to expand, and Old Town had to go. So Bovey moved it to the Nevada City site. Even if the buildings seen today were not built right here, they all are authentic Montana frontier structures whose histories have been documented.

LAURIN (PRONOUNCED *LOW-ray*) WAS the site of an 1863 gold strike that briefly convinced prospectors it was the new El Dorado. During the years of dredging on Alder Gulch, profits from a

machine digging at Laurin went into the coffers of Harvard University. In 1902, the town was prosperous enough to built a sturdy brick Catholic church, but by the 1930s only forty-five souls called Laurin home.

A little way from town is a cottonwood tree where Vigilantes ended the lives of two of Sheriff Plummer's gang in January 1864. When captured by the Vigilantes, Erastus Yager (known as "Red" for his hair and beard) freely admitted he was part of the gang, but stated that he'd never murdered anyone. He told the men that Plummer was head of the gang

(confirming their suspicions), named twenty additional members, explained that their password was "innocent" and that they all tied their bandanas in sailor's knots. Red said his only wish was that he could be held prisoner till the others had been hanged, but said he was glad that the committee was at work. His last words were, "Good-by, boys, you're on a good undertaking. God bless you." George Brown, the other desperado and the Innocents' secretary (whatever that might be), was nowhere near as stoical, but his frantic pleadings made no difference to the grim Vigilantes.

If it would make no particular difference to the authorities, the citizens would feel greatly obliged by the institution of a "rogue's corner," or malefactors' cemetery, where the professional gentleman [*sic*] of the road can keep each other company, without mingling their dust with the remains of honest citizens. The public feeling is very strong on this point, end [*sic*] we hear of one intended removal of a corpse to another locality.

(Virginia City)
Montana Post
October 7, 1865

Today's visitors to Virginia City notice, indeed, how the bad guys' section of the cemetery—"Boot Hill"—is separated from the larger portion.

PETE DALY'S, NEAR LAURIN, WAS A stagecoach stop where passengers could refresh themselves. It offered a saloon downstairs and a dance hall upstairs. Today it's known as "Robbers' Roost" because of one particular clientele: Red Yager's compadres, the road agents.

With Yager's information, the Vigilantes arrested the false sheriff, ignored Plummer's crying and promises to leave town at once, and hanged him. More hangings and banishments—accomplished with ominous warning notes—ended the area's worst crime problem.

BRANDON SPRANG TO LIFE AT THE mouth of Mill Creek in 1864, by fall boasting the Brandon City House hotel, twenty-seven cabins, and two blacksmith shops. The water-powered, twelve-stamp Brandon Mill opened the following year. The town's prosperity peaked in the early 1900s, mostly from employment in underground mines.

Although the Buckeye Mine lode was discovered in those early years, it wasn't developed until the 1880s, and a vein of galena (lead-producing ore) soon was located. The Buckeye Mine became one of Montana's greatest galena sources,

but the price of lead caused shutdowns of greater and lesser length, and it has been closed since 1983. The Toledo (originally Toleda) Mine and mill near Brandon also produced galena beginning in 1888, and was called the most active mine in its district in 1914.

At top, left and right: Robbers' Roost—Pete Daly's stage station— still stands. Occupants in later years added a turnstile and requested an admission "tip."

Above: Henry Plummer's Colt dragoon revolver, and leg irons from Bannack.
MONTANA HISTORICAL SOCIETY

Left: Once-hopeful Brandon City.

FLINT CREEK

Philipsburg is very much a living town, a lively county seat built on a rich mountainside along Flint Creek, its older structures testifying how rich were the surrounding sources of mainly gold and silver. Philipsburg is the grande dame who settled and survived long after the surrounding flamboyant floozies arrived and fled. Even Philipsburg's name, like its beginnings, comes from mining.

Above: Granite residents turn out for their Fourth of July parade around 1900. X's mark carriages and storefront of the Granite-Philipsburg stage line.
MONTANA HISTORICAL SOCIETY

Below: At Hasmark.

Hasmark, Tower, Granite, Rumsey, Kirkville

Hector Horton was prospecting Flint Creek in 1865 when he started noticing all the quartz outcroppings, which were rich in silver. He staked a claim, wintered over, then went to Silver Bow (future Butte) and talked about it. Other prospectors responded in proper stampede mode, and some of the most important claims in the area were staked out in 1866.

Among the first claims were the East Comanche and the Algonquin mines, served by a ten-stamp mill, but they weren't really developed until after 1877, when Philadelphia capital created the

Left: The eighty-stamp Algonquin Mill at Hasmark.

developers and now a Hauser partner, and transferred an experienced manager from their Argenta smelter to the new Stuart Mill. Philip Deidesheimer was his name, and he had prospered at Nevada's Comstock Lode, where he created the square-set method of timbering underground mines. St.L&M also bore the high cost of cutting a road up the hill.

In July, a settlement began to grow around the mill, and it soon was named Philipsburg after the manager. Miners joked that this name tripped off the tongue more easily than "Deidesheimersburg." At the end of 1867, Philipsburg boasted 1,500 souls living in 250 houses and served by six general stores, a newspaper, two doctors, three livery stables, Dana's Hotel, three blacksmiths, two breweries, and seven saloons. The Masonic fraternity was represented well and wealthily, erecting a lodge building for $6,000 (about $67,000 in today's money).

...considerable speculation in claims is going on in the Georgetown district.

(Virginia City)
Montana Post
Jan. 4, 1868

Hasmark was superseded by Philipsburg by the time this steel engraving of the Algonquin Mill was made.
MONTANA HISTORICAL SOCIETY

to the mill. The mill was expanded to 80 stamps, and treated a half million dollars' worth of ore in 1882–1883, including ore from the Granite Mountain Mine. By 1897, though, Hasmark had dwindled to the point of losing its post office.

World War I breathed new life into the Algonquin Mine, because its ore also included manganese. Germany had been the main supplier of this metal used in iron and steel processing, but now America needed its own supply. First one manganese mill, then a second and more efficient one, were built nearby; three more were added to process ore from forty area mines (especially the Trout Mill at Tower), a total of 200,000 tons from 1916 to 1918. After the war, the relatively low quality manganese ore couldn't compete economically in the steel market, but found some sales for dry-cell battery production. The Algonquin ran for eight years between 1923 and 1939.

Algonquin Company. Two years later, its employees found a richer vein, and the company put in the twenty-stamp Algonquin Mill. There the town of Hasmark arose, laid out along one straight, wide street lined by "tasteful and well designed cottages," as a resident wrote in 1879, an assay office, storehouses for mine supplies and for the tons of salt needed in ore refining. Chinese miners, he said, lived in a utilitarian company boarding house close

AS HASMARK'S DEVELOPMENT HAD begun, so had that of another town a few miles west. Samuel T. Hauser's St. Louis & Montana Mining Company bought rights to the Hope and Comanche lodes, two of the area's best. The St.L&M built a smelter named after James Stuart, one of the Gold Creek

Above: Philipsburg's Hope Mill dated from 1867, and originally was the Stuart Mill.
MONTANA HISTORICAL SOCIETY

Facing page top: An abandoned toy and buildings at Tower.

Facing page bottom: Remains of a flume, and a Tower blacksmith shop.

Ore from the Hope Lode kept the Stuart Mill's ten 650-pound, steam-powered stamps going. In 1867, St.L&M reorganized as Hope Mining Company and converted the mill to chloride processing—and its name to Hope Mill. The process didn't work well enough for the low silver values in this ore, and it also depended upon having tons of salt shipped from Salt Lake City. When the price of salt nearly tripled in only two years, investors shut down the mill.

Philipsburg emptied out—to a population of three.

SEPARATE LESSEES IN 1870 AND 1871 started the mill back to life, but Congress helped more in 1872, when it greatly increased the allowed size of a quartz-lode claim. The Speckled Trout lode a mile east of town attracted the attention of A. B. Nettleton, who partnered with James K. Pardee and Philadelphians who included Charlemagne Tower to create the North-West Company. The company bought four mines, then erected a $100,000 mill in 1875. Since the mill was fed mainly by the Speckled Trout Mine, it was known as the Trout Mill. Soon twenty cabins clustered around the

mill, and residents called the place Troutville for a while. When the North-West Company expanded Troutville as a liquor-free company town, they named it Tower in Charlemagne's honor.

Nearby Philipsburg came back to life as Tower grew, and then boomed as the district's center from 1881 to 1897. The Hope Mill no longer had to await ore from as far away as Black Pine. Railroad lines to Drummond (1883) and then a spur right into Philipsburg (1887) cut freighting costs for processed ore. McDonald's Opera House (refurbished in the 1990s and now back in use) was

SILVER BRICKS. We saw… at Dance, Stuart & Company's, a huge pile of silver bricks, of the estimated value of $10,000 in gold coin. They were produced at the Stuart mill, Philipsburg.… There are four mills running in [Montana] Territory that produce in the aggregate over $100,000 per month, and done so for many months past.

(Deer Lodge)
Weekly Independent
Oct. 24, 1868

Left: Granite's Miners' Union Hall.

Below: Granite Mountain Mill.

among two hotels, two banks, and other businesses built then.

BUT IT WAS THE TOWN OF GRANITE that had the biggest rollercoaster ride of the district's camps, with an amazing "ending" followed by a series of comebacks. During its heyday, "Montana's Silver Queen," four miles up Granite Mountain and slightly southeast of Philipsburg, competed as the area's most prominent town.

Granite's silver first was found when Eli D. Holland was hunting early in July 1875. Following an animal he had wounded, he came upon ore that, when he assayed down in Philipsburg, proved to be rich. But for five years nothing much happened with the shaft dug at the site. Then, Hope Mill superintendent Charles D. McClure picked up a piece of ore off the dump and discovered it assayed at a stunning 2,000 ounces of silver per ton. He promptly partnered with Charles Clark (no relation to the Butte "Copper King" family), and they collected $10 million in capital from St. Louis investors. The Granite Mountain Mining Company spent $130,000 from 1880 to 1882 to develop their Granite Mountain Mine. In 1882, miners who had dug through barren rock hit a lode and named it the Bonanza Chute. It was nearly as rich as the sample McClure had found. Investors began to receive dividends in 1885.

The company rented town lots for miners to build homes on, and soon Granite included Finnlander Lane and Cornish Row, while Donegal Lane was home to the Irish and and a few Danes. Magnolia Avenue's homes for the families of professional men were promptly nicknamed "Silk Stocking Row." The high, rocky townsite had no water, so

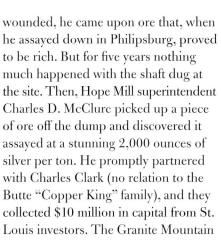

Above: Granite Mountain Mine superintendent's house.

Left: Cornish Row and Whiskey Hill, Granite.

MONTANA HISTORICAL SOCIETY

Right: The Granite Mountain Mill rises above Magnolia Avenue, Granite.
MONTANA HISTORICAL SOCIETY

Below: Granite.

at first it was hauled several miles from Fred Burr Lake, until a flume and cistern system were built. The business district included several banks, and Granite had four churches and one school. A bath house and a hospital served miners' lesser and greater needs. The *Granite Mountain Star* newspaper kept residents informed.

For entertainment there were a roller-skating rink, the lodges of three fraternal orders, and traveling theater companies in the auditorium of the Miners' Union Hall, which also housed pool tables on its ground floor and "the Northwest's

finest dancing floor" on its second. In winter, bold souls could bobsled down the hill to Philipsburg, but they had to trudge back up to Granite while a passing freight wagon obligingly pulled the sled. Across the street from Miners' Union Hall stood eighteen saloons, which fronted busy brothels.

Granite never had a cemetery because the ground was rock, so the departed were transported down Granite Mountain to Philipsburg's burying ground. From 1891 to 1893, they included an average of three men a year who died in mine accidents.

The Granite Mountain Mine sent 400 tons of ore to the Hope Mill in 1881, and 1,400 tons to the Algonquin Mill at Hasmark in 1882–1883. Then Granite Mountain Mining built its own twenty-stamp mill in 1885, and soon had to erect a second one, with eighty stamps. Ore production continued to outgrow milling capacity.

The company then built a ninety- or 100-stamp mill, operational in March 1889, which received ore from Granite Mountain Mine by an 8,900-foot tramway. Named the Rumsey Mill after the company president, the mill soon

Above: A ball mill survives at the Bimetallic Mine site; heavy steel balls inside the drum crushed ore.

Right: Granite Bank's vault.

Far left: Miners' Union Day parade through downtown Granite, around 1890.

Left: Tramway tower, Granite.

Below: Foundation of the mill at Rumsey.

was surrounded by a camp called Rumsey, home to 500 miners, mill workers, and their families. From Rumsey, a tunnel nearly as long as the tramway was dug into the Granite Mountain Mine, which produced $4 million in gold and silver in 1890. Granite Mountain Mining ran the operation until the Silver Purchase Act was repealed in 1893.

When another rich lode—the James G. Blaine—had been discovered on Granite Mountain in 1881, Hope Mill superintendent McClure snapped up the claim with his own money. He offered to sell it to his Granite Mountain Mining

partners at cost—$1,200—but the majority refused. McClure then incorporated the Bimetallic Mining Company, with Charles Clark and J. M. Merrell as partners, in 1886; its ownership overlapped with Granite Mountain Mining's by 80 percent, but it was a separate company for ten years.

Bimetallic built a fifty-stamp mill and mine offices on Douglas Creek a mile south of Philipsburg, at what first was known as Kirkville and then later as Clark. The mill opened in the first month of 1889 and was doubled in size only two years later. To connect it with the Blaine

lode, Bimetallic at first built a two-mile-long tramway whose buckets carried 500 pounds of ore down the mountain at a time, returning filled with fuel. The company began digging a tunnel into the mountain from the mill site, to enter the Blaine lode at its 1,000-foot depth.

For the World's Fair at Chicago in 1893, the Bimetallic sent a 4,307-pound bar of silver bullion to showcase the area's riches. By the time the Silver Purchase Act was repealed that summer and silver prices plummeted, the Bimetallic had made nearly a $13.8 million profit for its investors.

Above: Kirkville's combined Bimetallic Mill office and miners' lodging house.

Left: Kirkville.

*Right: Site of the mill that served Gr....
Bimetallic Consolidated, the world's largest
silver mine at the turn of the 20th century.*

Below: Water supply for Kirkville.

As of July 31, 1893, the federal government no longer had to purchase domestic silver. The next day, Granite Mountain Mining's mill engineer tied open the mill's steam whistle to announce shut-down. Within twenty-four hours, Granite town residents had left with what possessions they could transport. The Bimetallic ran another month before closing. Its tunnel from Douglas Creek was only a hundred feet from completion.

But the area's ghost-town status wasn't permanent—yet. In 1896, Granite Mountain Mining and Bimetallic Mining, with their overlapping ownership, were joined into a new corporation, Granite-Bimetallic Consolidated. This turned the holdings into the world's largest silver mine, and from 1898 to 1901 the lodes produced $1 million in bullion annually. The company also built a concentrator at the Bimetallic shaft to process old tailings along with lower-quality ore.

To mine more economically, the owners turned to electricity. Their subsidiary, Montana Water, Electric Power & Mining Company, took over a dam started on Flint Creek in 1890 and com-

pleted it in 1900. The water turned Georgetown Flats into Georgetown Lake, and the dam's 1,100 kilowatts ran Consolidated's mines and also went to area towns. Beginning in 1906, Consolidated sold power to Anaconda's Washoe smelter, and three years later sold the smelter the dam itself.

Consolidated suffered a layoff in 1905 when silver prices dropped, but miners were kept digging down through Granite Mountain. By 1913, they were working below water level, and the veins were far poorer, but the mountain still gave up $7.5 million in

ore from 1907 to 1932. The Consolidated closed in 1933, but reopened the following year long enough for a small crew to process 30,000 tons of ore.

Then it closed until 1958, when American Machine & Metal Corporation began to assess the old shafts. A fire that began in the surface engine room destroyed most of the town of Granite, but the exploratory crew were rescued from below ground.

Estimated total production of silver, and some gold, from the combined Granite and Bimetallic operations is more than $32 million.

…The Flint Creek silver mines have probably become as favorably and widely known in as short a space of time as those of Washoe in the '60s.…

*(Virginia City)
Montana Post*
Oct. 26, 1867

Right: Kirkville.

Left and bottom: The Sunrise Mine office and boarding house on Henderson Creek in 1997 and in 2000.

Below: A jaw crusher, for breaking rock into smaller pieces, at the Sunrise Mill.

Henderson, Black Pine, Combination

Joe Henderson found placer gold to the northwest in 1865, and saw his name placed on that gold-bearing creek, its gulch, and the mountain above. When he told the boys in Silver Bow about it the next year, they promptly joined him in sluicing, hydraulicking, and drift mining. The free gold lasted for about five years and amounted to about $300,000. After the first restless fortune-seekers moved on, Chinese miners came in to rework the tailings with care.

A dragline dredge was put into Henderson Creek in 1939 to reap gold. It had dug $18,000 worth when nonessential gold mining was stopped for World War II. From 1943 to 1946, a connected-bucket dredge was allowed to operate here because it also collected sheelite, an ore that was 63 percent tungsten (used to harden steel). Henderson Creek's tungsten concentrates from these years were worth more than $450,000.

Some of Henderson Gulch's placer gold came from the lode low on Sunrise Mountain that was exploited by the Queen, Sunrise, and Russell mines, which ran from 1892 to 1903. That ore was taken down to Henderson Gulch by both gravity and level trams or by ore chute, where processing retrieved $4 to $10 of gold per ton in the Henderson Mill below the Queen Mine. Soon the settlement of—yes—Henderson huddled around the mill, but the low-level ore and the town were finished by 1907.

RESTLESS PROSPECTORS MAY HAVE done a little hard rock silver mining atop the ridge between lower Willow Creek and Smart Creek in the 1870s, but the area's thick timber helped protect it. People who owned the claims didn't find them worth developing until the early 1880s, when 400 tons of ore went to the Hope Mill in Philipsburg and gave up 77¢ in silver per ton. By 1885, the Black Pine Mining Company's six owners had bought many area claims, created rough and twisting roads, and begun development.

Shortly after the Black Pine Mine reopened in 1891, two miners were killed in accidents five months apart. Then the mine closed in 1893 after passage of the Silver Purchase Act, leaving its 130 miners without jobs. There was some gold in the ore, so the company decided to reopen, but that lasted only until 1897.

Right and bottom: Gold Hill Mine, Princeton.

On the ridge itself, a settlement called Black Pine grew around the mine. In 1889, a forest fire destroyed the town's fifty buildings and mine structures. The new company town that was built by 1891 had a single street with cabins, a boarding house, and mine offices. Stable family men were wanted, and so saloons and other such amusements were forbidden. Of course, a cluster of just such businesses—called Whiskey Hill—sprang up beyond the company's property line. Whiskey Hill buildings were torn down in the 1950s by the landowner, and in 1988 the Combination Fire passed through and destroyed Black Pine down to its foundations and two headframes.

THE BLACK PINE MINING COMPANY'S most promising lead was the Combination Mine, where they employed eighty men. Beginning in 1887, multi-horse teams pulled ore-filled wagons two miles down the dangerous mountainside to the company's ten-stamp silver mill on Willow Creek. The concentrated ore then traveled on to the Hope Mill via eighteen-horse pack strings.

Just as miners in the Combination started digging into high-grade ore, Black Pine Mining stockholders rebelled at losing money because of land clearing and road construction. After they cut off funds, the mine's structures were sold at sheriff's sale. Some of the original owners repurchased the property and formed the Combination Mining & Milling Company, focused on that mine.

When the mill began running again in mid-1888, the ore averaged nearly $23 in silver per ton. Three years later, the mill was doubled to twenty stamps. The company erected Combination, a small company town, at the mill.

World War II brought tungsten mining to the Combination Mine also; its ore was 21 percent tungsten, less valuable than nearby Princeton's.

Princeton

Northeast of Granite, on Boulder Creek (a tributary of Flint Creek), sat Princeton, center for late 19th and early 20th century lode mining. The first lode was found here in 1868, but by the time the three discovering miners sought capital for greater development, the

Panic of 1873 limited investors; then Philipsburg's and Granite's booms made the Princeton area less interesting. In the 1880s, though, a French company got mining underway here, and others followed.

The Nonpareil Mine on Boulder Creek was active from 1891 to 1893, with mostly silver and lead, plus a little gold, running to 280 feet below surface. Production totaled about $50,000.

Gold and a little silver came out of the five shafts of Gold Hill Mine atop a ridge above South Boulder Creek. Its mill processed a few hundred tons of ore, but was inefficient for the values.

Amputation.—Some two months ago, Mr. Wm. Dingwell, while hunting stock in the Flint Creek Hills, had his feet badly frozen. At the time he wore short-legged gum boots, and the snow getting into them, melted and froze his feet fast to the boots. When he reached a house the boots had to be cut from his feet. He was taken to Henderson gulch, where he received the best of attention, and for a long time it was hoped that he would recover. On Saturday last Dr. J.S. Glick was called to his assistance. It was found necessary to amputate the left leg above the ankle, but the patient being very low it was deemed advisable to defer operations on the right foot...As soon as it can be done with safety, his right leg will be amputated.

(Deer Lodge)
Weekly Independent
Feb. 3, 1872

Both were closed by 1913.

The Brooklyn Mine drove 600 feet deep, two miles from Princeton up Pierre Hill. Records of earlier production are lost, but in 1907–1909 its ore ran 37 ounces of silver per ton, with some zinc and lead and a small amount of copper. It was closed until 1914, then worked until 1918 and off and on during the 1920s. A zinc concentrator was built in 1915. The Brooklyn Consolidated Mines Co. took over in 1935, putting six miners underground and building a ball mill, powerhouse, blacksmith shop, eight log cabins and a boarding house,

and two barns. They closed that same year, then the mine was reopened in 1938 and stayed active into the 1940s.

Alps Mining District

The late boom here, in 1895, was a real firecracker, with 2,000 people rushing to the mouth of Brewster Creek on Rock Creek. Even then-President Grover Cleveland invested $1.5 million in the district's development, which included digging three mines, building

a stamp mill, grading twelve miles of railroad bed to connect with the Northern Pacific, and creating an aqueduct—all because people had heard that a carload of ore from this area west of Ophir held incredibly rich gold values.

In a year, it was all over except for the Golconda Mine, where eleven miners still were employed. The rumors of great wealth, in the slang of the day, had been a "humbug."

Georgetown, Southern Cross, Red Lion, Gold Coin

Prospectors showed up on Georgetown Flats by Flint Creek near the beginning of Montana Territory's gold rush, in 1866, and area placers produced $40,000 in the next four years. Some men tried hydraulicking and a bit of lode mining, but the quartz lodes were low grade. The camp called Georgetown was abandoned by 1886, and fourteen years later was inundated by the creation of Georgetown Lake.

A COUPLE MILES NORTH OF GEORGEtown lay Southern Cross, a mining camp named by a sailor for the constellation

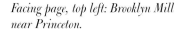

Facing page, top left: Brooklyn Mill near Princeton.

Facing page, top right: The view into an Alps Mining District mine tunnel.

Facing page, bottom: In the Alps district.

Southern Cross: shaft house (top); mine offices (top right); boarding house (right).

Center: Red Lion.

Above: The Gold Coin Mine.

viewable only from Earth's southern hemisphere. The Southern Cross Mine held quartz gold found in 1866. It was not developed until the early 1870s. After first sending its ore to East Helena, then building an inefficient on-site mill, owner Salton Cameron settled on sending the ore to the Washoe Smelter in Anaconda for processing. Cameron made good money, but the mine's richest vein wasn't located until 1904, by lessee Lucian Eaves. The mine, purchased by Anaconda Copper Mining in 1910, is estimated to have produced $5 million in gold, silver, and copper.

NORTHEAST OF GEORGETOWN LAKE and difficult to reach was the Red Lion lode, developed in the late 1880s. An inefficient ten-stamp mill built for mines digging the lode in 1891 lost about half the ore's gold value, and production totaled around $38,000 in gold by the time the facilities were dismantled in 1906.

THE GOLD COIN LODE WAS discovered in 1898, and produced $200,000 in gold over the next ten years. Its namesake mill opened in 1906, running until 1909 and again in 1912. From 1930 to 1940 fifteen miners worked the Gold Coin Mine, sending out ore worth $140,000.

PIONEER MOUNTAINS

A correspondent from Bannack reported:

From this time the course of [Argenta] is upward and onward. Two years ago, only a few laborious and care worn prospectors might be seen here and there with pick and shovel, walking over the hills, some of them poor indeed, living in mere hovels and caves, but they had faith in the country, and we trust, yes, we believe that their fondest hopes and fanciful dreams will yet be more than realized.

[Argenta] now has her stores and shops, boarding and public houses, and the weary traveller can find good "round meals" for himself and horse at Frank Esler's whose lady knows how to make the wayfaring man at home.

(Virginia City)
Montana Post
Oct. 6, 1866

Here is Montana's land of argentum—silver—in veins so rich they vied respectably with Nevada's Comstock Lode. Isolated company towns housed hardrock miners, smeltermen, and their families, trying to offer comforts and amenities in the middle of nowhere. Capitalists whose investments funded development were the ones who reaped the big profits—or who, like William Allen, spent their lifetimes trying to recover what had been lost.

Above: Lower Main Street in Glendale, around 1882.
MONTANA HISTORICAL SOCIETY

Below: Ermont Mine development began late, in 1926.

Argenta, Farlin, Vipond Park, Ermont

Argenta's riches were first seen shortly after Bannack's in 1862, by placer miners who pushed into the Pioneer Mountains when claims on Grasshopper Creek became scarce. But the town's short life existed separately from those of interconnected Bannack and Virginia City, with their overlapping Vigilantes and founding citizens. Argenta didn't have much placer gold, and development really began on two days in June 1864, when William Beekan, Charles S. Ream, and J. A. Brown located seven silver mines. They named this the Montana Mining District. The next January, the town of Montana was chartered here at the headwaters of

Right: Northernmost of the Ermont Mines.

Below: Argenta mine shaft.

Bottom: Argenta, with Montana Territory's first silver amalgamation mill, received ore from around southwestern Montana.

Rattlesnake Creek, but in 1867, it became Argenta, from the Latin for silver.

In 1865, A. M. Esler opened the mine he named the Legal Tender, which had such rich silver ore that at least one shipment went by boat to a smelter in Swansea, Wales, for processing. While the other mines didn't justify that kind of freight expense, they were good producers. All they needed was a nearby smelter.

Samuel T. Hauser, more businessman than mining gambler, went home to St. Louis in 1865 and tapped family and friends as investors in his St. Louis & Montana Mining Company (St.L&M). He came back to Montana followed by smelter equipment and fire brick shipped up the Missouri to Fort Benton, then freighted overland to Argenta. In 1866, the company opened Montana

Territory's first silver amalgamation mill and contracted to treat Legal Tender ore. The smelter stood for a century.

St.L&M had the mill built and then supervised by a German, August Steitz, who drew on his nation's advanced technology. When he became ill in 1866 or 1867, he was replaced by Philip Deidesheimer, who had learned his chops at the United State's premier silver mine, Nevada's Comstock Lode. Hauser and partner James Stuart also bought six mining claims in the Argenta area.

S. H. Bohm Company, of Helena, bought and enlarged the smelter in 1870, and treated ore from Moose Creek and Vipond Park, among other districts. Esler built his own small smelter for the Legal Tender in 1866, having to sell most of his interest in the mine to get the money; could it be he didn't like seeing St.L&M make money from his mine? At least two more smelters were built in the district, including one that future copper king William A. Clark purchased in 1869 and operated into the early 1890s.

Argenta's lodes began to play out in the early 1870s, and miners began to

Right: Sod-roofed schoolhouse at Farlin.

move on. The smelters worked on lower-grade ores until the Panic of 1873 lowered silver prices. By the time the nation had recovered from that depression, Glendale and East Helena had much more efficient smelters than Argenta's.

THE FARLIN BROTHERS, O. D. (SOME records list George W.) and W. L., recorded their Indian Queen Mine north of Argenta on Christmas Eve, 1875. O. D. (or was it George?) had made another claim here nine years before, but the whole district had been ignored since then. And it was again, until the 1880s,

Argenta grew considerably over its first winter, as a correspondent was pleased to announce.

…Last September the town [Argenta] contained but one store, which also served as a meat market, post office, and hotel. The St. Louis and Montana Smelting works, were not yet completed. Now, we have three large establishments containing a generous assortment of goods, three restaurants and hotels, two saloons, a billiard room, blacksmiths, baker, butcher, tailor and shoemaker shops. The buildings are either frame or hewn timber, and present a very respectable appearance.

(Virginia City)
Montana Post
Feb. 23, 1867

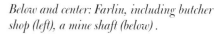

The building of a brewery in Argenta by German brothers named Beehrer caused a correspondent to the *Montana Post* to wax philosophical, but not grammatical, on how different cultures settled in new lands:

…The Spaniard builds first a church, the Yankee a school house, the German a brewery; and in this mountain land of ours, the last is scarcely the least in importance, if it but accomplish its task, and substitutes lager for the compounds infernal, which are drank as liquor.

(Virginia City)
Montana Post
April 6, 1867

when iron ore was dug for processing use by Hecla Consolidated at Glendale.

The Indian Queen Mine was reopened, and development began in the late 1890s under a series of corporations. The third of them, Western Mining Company, built a blast furnace to process the mine's ore. Workers and miners who settled around it named their community Farlin. Its boom years were 1905 and 1906, when the Indian Queen produced half a million pounds of copper (along with 16,000 ounces of silver and 160 of gold); the Anaconda Copper Mining Company took notice; and Farlin briefly had its

own post office. But ore quality went down from then until the mine closed in 1923, only having tripled those first two years' copper and silver production.

AT THE NORTHEASTERN END OF THE Pioneers were Vipond Park, 8,000 feet in elevation, and the Quartz Hill Mining District, site of the Quartz Hill and other rich silver mines, led by the Lone Pine Mine.

John Vipond found the first lode in 1868, but getting the ore down and out for processing was the problem. He and his brother William had earlier run a grocery in German Gulch, southeast of

Above: At Vipond, an ore chute has been buried by sediment sliding downhill.

Center: Wickes.

Left: Farlin.

Right: Vipond.

Below: An Ermont Mine adit.

Above: The Lone Pine concentrating mill.

Right: Collapsed adit at Quartz Hill.

Georgetown Lake. Finally in 1872, area miners—including a third Vipond brother, Joseph—built their own road north to the town of Dewey, where they could connect with the road to the Union Pacific railhead at Corinne, Utah. Later, Dewey boasted three silver mills.

Washington Black, a freight hauler under contract to the Vipond Park mines, took the first load of ore to Utah over that road. He was still hauling freight seventeen years later when he made the discovery in what became the Quartz Hill district. Seeing loose silver ore on the surface in June 1889, he loaded his wagon full.

The Vipond Park and Quartz Hill districts together produced more than a million ounces of silver, and more than a thousand of gold, along with other metals—and that's only what was recorded from 1902, when surviving records begin, through 1965.

THE ERMONT SUB-DISTRICT OF THE Argenta Mining District was the site of one of the last gold rushes in the United States, when artificially high gold prices during the Great Depression inspired out-of-work men to come prospecting.

The first gold was not found here

[At Quartz Hill] we took a look at the quartz lodes… The "Williamson" is the best developed…, having a shaft down about forty feet…Much credit is due to the prospectors…for the energy displayed in bringing to light these hidden veins of wealth. We hope they will receive their reward, or at least a part of it, in this world.

(Virginia City)
Montana Post
Oct. 5, 1867

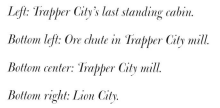

Left: *Trapper City's last standing cabin.*

Bottom left: *Ore chute in Trapper City mill.*

Bottom center: *Trapper City mill.*

Bottom right: *Lion City.*

until 1926, by D. V. Erwin and W. J. Corbett, who began to develop their shallow (110-foot) Ermont Mine the next year. In 1932, gold prospectors staked out thirty-three claims in the surrounding area. Erwin and Corbett sold the Ermont to R. B. Caswell, J. R. Bowles and F. C. Gram, who also bought the other claims. They mined off and on until 1936, when they built an electric-powered, 100-ton stamp mill. Until 1942, the mill ran around the clock and employed sixty men whose production totalled $22,000 a month. After the war, the Ermont properties ran from time to time until the 1960s.

Trapper City, Lion City, Glendale, Hecla

Hecla Mining District's four towns were strung out along ten miles of gulches reaching up the side of Lion Mountain, served by charcoal kilns located on the other side. Each town developed its own character, small as they were.

Prospectors first marked claims in the area in 1872, but did nothing more. The next summer, four miners from Vipond came into the area hunting for meat (and,

of course, prospecting as they went). One of them, James A. Bryant, wanted to relocate a claim he'd made on Trapper Ridge the year before. The mining district that developed was named for him.

The weather was hot, and the flies so overpowering that the men's horses stampeded to escape the biting. As they searched for the horses, P. J. (Jerry) Grotevant came on a vein of ore right on the surface. While they awaited its assay, the men staked claims and went to work. They had struck a rich silver and lead lode at the head of Trapper Creek. Bryant and friends took the first ore out

GOLD VERSUS SILVER

During the last quarter of the 19th century, the terms "free silver" and "gold standard" were fighting words around the United States, not just in the West's silver-producing states. They were slogans for complicated issues the nation faced, as it moved from a farming economy to an industrial one and suffered a series of financial "panics" (recessions and depressions) that caused bank failures and personal bankruptcies.

For Montana Territory, what was called "the silver issue" arose right when Montanans needed investors to support hard-rock mining development. Montana's placer gold rushes were over, and the state's miners and those who depended on them all wanted to see hard-rock mines dug and supplied with equipment. That took capital.

And the capitalists—owners and stockholders—were in business to make money. If they invested in mines, they wanted to sell the metals at good prices. Since gold and silver were used to make coins, whether the U.S. and other governments were buying the metals was very important.

In the years after the Civil War, the entire nation was concerned about economic policy, and followed the issues closely. During this time, two laws—first one, then the other—shaped the market for silver and gold.

In Montana, they also shaped the boom and then the bust that created so many of the ghost towns in this book.

One of many questions in the national economic debate was: What stood behind our paper currency and coins? Four main points of view developed about how to back currency: by a federal stock of gold bullion; by the same stock in silver; by both gold and silver in national vaults; or by nothing more than the honorable word of the national government.

The last opinion, represented by the Greenback Party, didn't get as far as the others, but the party did run candidates for President of the United States in 1876, 1880, and 1884 before fading away. Many thoughtful planks in its platform later were adopted by major parties, such as child-labor prohibition.

Those who favored the gold standard faced off with those who favored the silver standard. Gold was becoming scarcer in the United States, but

the West still had plenty of silver to mine. More silver standard advocates lived in the West, where Montana followed only Colorado in value of silver production. In the 1880s, silver mining was Montana's greatest industry, and in 1887 Montana Territory beat even Colorado's output.

An important feature of the gold standard was that it represented "tight" money—fewer dollars in circulation, with a dollar's value staying at the same level. Free silver and unlimited silver advocates said that more dollars in circulation meant it was easier for farmers and others with long-term loans to pay them off.

Gold bullion. The card reads: June 2, 1904/1766 Ounces Bullion/ Value/$31,788⁰⁰/From a 27-day Run/Barnes-King Mill/Kendall, Mont.

MONTANA HISTORICAL SOCIETY

The "bimetallists" thought that currency supported by both gold and silver made sense in a nation that had natural supplies of both. That had been how things worked before the Civil War, when the federal government purchased both metals for coins. It issued dollar-value coins made of either metal, but guaranteed that 16 silver dollars were issued for each gold dollar. This was "free silver" coinage.

In 1878, bimetallists U.S. Rep. Richard Bland drafted, and Sen. William Allison amended, the bill that became known as the Bland-Allison Act. The federal government was required to buy $2 million to $4 million worth of silver every month, and coin it into silver dollars. Mints would turn out as many dollars as the purchased amount of silver created.

Supporters of the gold standard sought to repeal the Bland-Allison Act, while those who supported silver wanted to change it to eliminate the upper limit of $4 million purchased per month. They wanted "unlimited silver" coinage.

This struggle led to passage of Sen. John T. Sherman's Silver Purchase Act in 1890. Another compromise by bimetallists, it required the federal government to purchase and coin all the U.S.-produced silver it was offered. But the act also set the price of silver at market value—whatever dealers were willing to pay—and not at the old 16 to 1 ratio. When the law passed, silver's market price was low.

Of course, the price of silver rose as soon as the government had to buy it all. Now, investors were happier than ever to improve or develop their Montana silver mines. The brand-new state's economy boomed.

But the Sherman Silver Purchase Act didn't fix the nation's financial woes, which came from many factors beyond gold versus silver. In 1893, the act was repealed. Instantly, many Montana mines shut down, and miners and their families left to seek work elsewhere. Most dramatic was Granite, where the mine tied its steam whistle open as soon as the news arrived, and in twenty-four hours the town was nearly deserted.

Still debating the standard behind the U.S. dollar, the two major political parties focused on it in the presidential campaigns of 1896 and 1900. Both times the Democrats nominated William Jennings Bryan to run against William McKinley. Both times Bryan gave his dramatic stump speech that culminated in stating the gold standard would "crucify mankind upon a cross of gold." That is, "tight" dollars would harm the average farmer or worker more than the silver standard would. Both times McKinley won the presidency.

After 1900, improved economic conditions and other factors lessened national interest in the debate, and eventually the gold standard was formally adopted.

Montana's mining future would hinge on copper, as America embraced electricity—delivered via copper wiring—to light their homes and power their workplaces. Montana's next ghost town–creating bust would be that of dryland homesteading in the eastern part of the state, but that was three decades in the future.

VIPOND.—Mr. John Brannigan and others are trying to make arrangements to have smelting works erected near the rich lodes of this district. It is generally believed by those who are acquainted with the quality of ore and extent of quartz in Vipond, that at least 200 men will be in that vicinity as soon as fair weather opens.

(Deer Lodge)
Weekly Independent
Jan. 27, 1872

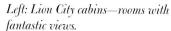
Left: Lion City cabins—rooms with fantastic views.

Below: The Lower Cleve Mine, Lion City.

Below center: Out these openings poured ore crushed by Trapper City stamps.

by pack train to a wagon road where it was loaded for the railroad at Corinne, Utah, and sent to Denver for smelting. Only four years later, in 1877, the discoverers sold their claims to the Hecla Consolidated Mining Company.

Of course, news of their finds created a rush in 1873. Joe McCreary, a friend of Grotevant, was prospecting here when he caught a glimpse of Grotevant's white mule and mistook it for a mountain lion. He ran back to camp in a lather over the sighting, which set him up for plenty of ribbing once things were straightened out. In fact, his fellow min-

ers took to calling the whole mountain "Lion" for McCreary's benefit, and so it remains to this day.

TRAPPER CITY, CHRONOLOGICALLY the first town, reached a population of from 200 to 1,000 souls, depending on the estimator. Built on Sappington Creek, it soon was largely abandoned as mining moved up onto Lion Mountain.

LION CITY, PARTWAY UP THE MOUNTAIN, featured log cabin homes and some frame buildings for mine offices, along with saloons and other mining-camp

Above: On the outskirts of Glendale.

Left: Elkhorn Mining Company stamps at Lion City.

Right: Hecla Mining Company superintendent Henry Knippenberg's "mansion" looked down over Glendale.
MONTANA HISTORICAL SOCIETY

Below: The only store building remaining in Glendale.

Center: Sad story in Glendale cemetery.

Bottom: The Canyon Creek charcoal kilns that made fuel for the Glendale smelter.

Right: Hecla Consolidated office building at Hecla, with smelter stack in background.

entertainments, from nymphs of the pavement to rigged games of chance to whiskey-fueled fistfights. Lion City blossomed to include 500 to 600 miners and those who served them.

GLENDALE, AT THE LOWER END OF the chain, began around a smelter built in 1875. In 1877, Noah Armstrong bought the best claims on Lion Mountain and created Hecla Consolidated Mining Company to develop them. The smelter burned in the summer of 1879, and a larger and better one was built on the site two years later by the new owners of Hecla Mining,

led by Henry Knippenberg, who bought out Armstrong that year of 1881. Glendale, the most sober, nonviolent, and "civilized" of the towns, was where Knippenberg built his family a frame mansion on the hillside above a short street lined by stone stores and office buildings. During the 1880s boom in the area, nearly 2,000 residents called Glendale home.

KNIPPENBERG, WHO SUPERINTENDED the mine, wanted to remove miners from the unholy opportunities too readily available in Lion City. So, he created the company town of Hecla at the top of the

I do believe that if a Cayuse [horse] trail was found leading to the infernal regions, a stampede would be got up there after gold...

[signed] "Friend" in (Virginia City) *Montana Post* Sept. 2, 1865

Left: Canyon Creek charcoal kilns.

Below and bottom: In Hecla.

mountain in 1881. Mine offices were moved there, and company boarding houses were built. Besides improving their morals, the lodgings let miners stay near work during the snowy weather, when climbing up and down the mountain wasn't too desirable.

The following year, Knippenberg added the Greenwood Concentrator halfway down the mountain. To transport the ore from mine to concentrator, the company laid four miles of rails down Lion Mountain. For year-round operation, they later added snowsheds to cover the tracks. Ore slid down loading chutes

from the mine into the cars. When three cars were full, a brakeman boarded the unpowered tram and released the brake for its gravity-pulled downhill run. His job was to keep the cars at a reasonable speed, but brakemen regularly were known to jump off when they thought the cars were getting beyond control.

To help power these two plants, Hecla Mining operated its own thirty-eight-kiln charcoal plant at Canyon Creek on the other side of Lion Mountain, where mostly Canadian and French loggers cut lodgepole pine and mostly Italian kiln operators reduced it to the concentrated fuel. Before

the kilns were built, they had stacked cordwood 12 feet high by 25 feet long, covered it with dirt, and set it afire to dry and carbonize slowly. While monitoring the lengthy process, the men had 12' x 12' cabins for shelter. Over the nineteen years that the Hecla smelter ran, Hecla loggers cut 11,665 acres of pines to produce 19 million bushels of charcoal.

Railroad service reaching into western Montana in the early 1880s greatly benefited the Hecla operations. After trains delivered coke and mining supplies, Knippenburg filled the empty cars with 90-pound bars of silver bullion that

Left: Fifteen tons of Hecla Mine ore heading for a smelter pass west of Twin Bridges in the 1890s.

MONTANA HISTORICAL SOCIETY

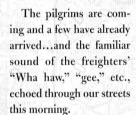

Right: The Glendale smelter in 1880 or 1881.
MONTANA HISTORICAL SOCIETY

Below: Lion Mountain's gravity-powered ore tram line.

Above: Elkhorn Mining Co. office building, which included Coolidge's post office.

Right: Coolidge.

he shipped to Omaha for final processing.

Hecla properties continued to produce even after 1893, when the price of silver dropped, but in 1900 the smelter at Glendale was closed and torn down. The last Hecla mine closed in 1904.

Henry Knippenberg remained convinced of the district's value, though, and bought the Hecla properties at sheriff's sale. Lessees operated some of his mines until 1915, and then slag piles were reworked and some mines operated by various owners and leasers into the 1960s.

From about twenty miles of tunnelling in Lion Mountain, the Bryant Mining District produced $22 million in silver and other metals.

Coolidge

Coolidge was a small company town created by a former politician, and site of Montana's final and largest silver development, which lasted less than two decades.

The Elkhorn Mining District sits at 7,000 to 8,000 feet in elevation, on the divide from which flow the Wise River and Bannack's Grasshopper Creek. Its silver was first found in 1872, and dozens of mines operated off and on for the rest of the 19th century, most successfully after railroad transport reached the area in the early 1880s. The district was asleep from

1893 until 1906, when a little mining began again.

Then along came William R. Allen, a Republican who had been elected Montana's lieutenant governor in 1908, at the age of thirty-seven. Born in French Gulch near Anaconda, Montana Territory, a graduate of the Helena Business College, he had worked for Marcus Daly managing non-mining corporations owned by the Anaconda Company: the rail line, electric plant and water works, a sheet metal plant, and the lumber business. Allen also inherited some mining interests from his father.

Allen's 20th-century version of prospecting was to create the Boston-Montana Development Corporation. He invested nearly half a million dollars of his own, and set it to buying up eighty claims in the Elkhorn Mining District. Although he had been reelected lieutenant governor in 1912, he quit politics permanently the next year to establish the company and its subsidiaries, the Boston-Montana Milling and Power Company (for the mill) and the Butte and Pacific Railway Company, which built a line from the district to meet the main rail lines at Divide.

Slowed by World War I, the railway connected in 1919. Then the heavy equipment could come in for mill construction, which took three years and nearly $1 million. The largest silver mill Montana had seen could process 750 tons of ore daily, recovering 90 percent or more of its silver. The resulting concentrate would be shipped to Tooele, Utah, and East Helena smelters.

Mill, mine, railroad, and town took $5 million to build—$41.6 million in today's money.

The town of Coolidge began to take shape in 1919 with tents on wooden platforms used as temporary housing for mill builders. Allen was said to have named it for his friend Calvin Coolidge, who had begun serving four years in the Massachusetts state senate while Allen was lieutenant governor out in Montana. It also was rumored that the future President was an investor in Boston-Montana.

By 1922, the town was a mixture of

Facing page, top left: The Coolidge stables.

Facing page, top right: Ore buckets from Coolidge's tramway.

Facing page, bottom left: Frank Tyro house in Coolidge.

Facing page, bottom right: William R. Allen.
MONTANA HISTORICAL SOCIETY

Right: Elkhorn Mine and Mill at Coolidge.

Below: Coolidge school house.

Below right: Trestle at the Upper Elkhorn Mine, near Coolidge.

primitive living and modern conveniences. It had electric lights and telephones, but most of the board-and-tarpaper houses were without plumbing—residents used the mill's showers. A company store was the only place to shop for food, miners' gear, and other goods. There was neither saloon nor church. Single miners could take their meals at a company boarding house.

A school opened in 1918 with twenty or so pupils, and Coolidge obtained a post office in 1922. Entertainment meant the pool hall, or skiing and sledding during the long winters. All the residents were Caucasian, with 250 men working in the mine and the mill.

At the mine itself, the "upper camp" held long cabins, bunkhouses, boarding house and cook house, carpenter and blacksmith shops, stables, and an ore-sorting building.

But as soon as the complex was ready to go, the national economy took a downturn and silver prices plunged. The mill never processed at peak capacity, and handled only 52,385 tons of ore from 1921 to 1925. It operated five different times from then through 1953, for a total production of just $375,000.

In 1923, the whole operation had gone into recceivership. W. R. Allen lost his personal fortune along with control of the property. Mining continued but there wasn't enough money to develop the amount of tunnelling needed to feed the mill. Then a Montana Power Company dam failed in 1927, its waters washing out twelve miles and several bridges of Boston-Montana's railroad.

William R. Allen spent the remaining years of his life, which ended in 1953, living in Wise River and trying to get the complex going again.

MOOSETOWN
HIGHLAND CITY
RED MOUNTAIN CITY
SILVER STAR
ROCHESTER
PARROT

A Rochester correspondent wrote the *Montana Post*:

Rochester gulch, which occasioned a big stampede last October, is still here, awaiting warm weather and "ye honest miner" to unearth its buried riches. Every indication tends to show this will be a good camp. At any rate, the quartz will compare favorably with the best.

(Virginia City)
Montana Post
Feb. 23, 1867

HIGHLAND MOUNTAINS & JEFFERSON RIVER

Slow and steady, Highland Mountains precious metal mines operated well into the 20th century, long after the placer gold had played out. The "cities" that were to be, stopped developing and faded away when railroads passed them by, but riches awaited in deep mines for those with the capital to develop them.

Above: Rochester in 1905.
MONTANA HISTORICAL SOCIETY

Below: Moosetown.

Moosetown, Highland City, Red Mountain City, Silver Star, Rochester

Moosetown on the Highland Mountains' Moose Creek, dating from 1866, was never more than a cluster of a few log cabins. Placer miners cleared up to $10 a day per man over the first five years. Then in 1872, placering produced only $2,000 total.

But three extremely rich lodes had been discovered in 1867, and they held as much as $400 in gold per ton of ore. They and other area lodes were worked until just before World War I.

LATE IN JULY OF 1866, THREE prospectors found gold in Fish Creek on Red Mountain in the Highlands, and the rush was on. As with the Moose Creek area, gold lodes were discovered almost at once; more than 100 were

located within the next three years.

Highland City and Red Mountain City came to life right beside each other, each with a population of 1,000 in 1867. Red Mountain City, then larger than Silver Bow (future Butte), even boasted a water system made of hollowed logs.

A miner named Ron D. Leggat became the district's magnate. He started with placering and turned to hydraulicking, then went on to buy the placer claims of miners who were moving on, which he mined hydraulically. He continued until 1895, when the Butte Water Company bought him out in order to protect the city's water supply.

Some area mines closed early in the 20th century, and others produced intermittently into the 1920s. When the Great Depression began, some Butte residents turned to Red Mountain and began placering and even lode mining. World War II restrictions closed these mines, but production later began again and continued into the early 1960s. Gold from around Highland and Red Mountain cities is estimated to have totalled $2.3 million, and small-scale placering continues.

SILVER STAR IN THE SOUTHEASTERN Highlands was born a few years after a man named Green Campbell located a quartz lode in 1867 and opened a mine he named for himself. Today the burg on the Jefferson River is another of Montana's not-really ghost towns. But for its first decade, Silver Star was the most important town between Virginia City and Helena. Green Campbell's mine operated until 1942, is estimated to have given up as many as 20,000 ounces of gold, and was only one of twenty-five free-milling quartz mines in the area. Another was Bill and George Boyer's Silver Star Mine, which began operating around 1869.

Above: At the Broadway Mine near Silver Star.

Top: Mill at Highland City.

THE ONLY CHANCE LODE, situated near Highland, is one of the very few lodes which has furnished its own expenses for prospecting, and in addition yielded a handsome profit to its owners....Mr. Stephenson, one of the fortunate owners in this very valuable property, informs us that the company design putting up a mill for early spring operations. They will take out quartz during the winter so as to be prepared for continuous operations during the next spring and summer.

(Deer Lodge) *Weekly Independent,* Sept. 18, 1868

The Masons at Red Mountain City are making Preparations for a Ball at that place, which bids fair to eclipse any thing of the kind that has ever transpired in that section....

(Deer Lodge) Weekly Independent, Jan. 16, 1869

Miners who discovered the Rochester lodes "have added a new and powerful link to the golden chain of Montana's greatness."

(Deer Lodge) *Weekly Independent,* March 13, 1869

FROM HIGHLAND

...Our city is looking upward at present. We have had for the past two months that stagnation of business that always befalls young mining camps, and from which they recover sooner or later, to go forward with renewed vigor and vitality. We are taking out considerable money from our placers, while more are being opened daily, and our quartz interests are promising better than that of any district in the Territory. Croakers may croak about the Territory being "played out," but we challenge any unbiased person to come here and carefully survey our future prospects, and go away with any other impression than that Highland gulch...has a brighter future (both political and pecuniary) than any other place of equal size in the Rocky Mountains.

(Virginia City) *Montana Post,* Aug. 31, 1867

MOOSE CREEK.—This mining district, situate[d] about six miles west of Red Mountain City, is now receiving considerable attention. The quartz found is silver bearing and bids fair to rival if it does not surpass any mining district in Montana. The ledges are of good width and the ore is rich....One hundred dollars per ton is the estimate that competent persons place upon the value of all the ore taken from this mine....

(Deer Lodge) *Weekly Independent,* Feb. 27, 1869

Red Mountain City—the town of Highland [Mining District]—has heretofore been in the strictest sense of the word a placer mining town, lively in summer and dull in winter. But hereafter…its mercantile demands and its business interests must follow suit and assume permanence likewise.

(Deer Lodge)
Weekly Independent
March 13, 1869

HIGHLAND GULCH:

Nearly 500 men are searching for its hidden riches, and many have been very successful. Bill Fairweather, (of course it is needless to say that he discovered Alder gulch,) was in town last Saturday and claimed that it is ten miles long; and equal in richness to his discovery.

(Virginia City)
Montana Post
Sept. 15, 1866

Soon two mining camps arose across the Jefferson from each other, connected at first only by a swinging footbridge. One was named Silver Star after the mine, and the other got the ignominious monicker of Ragtown. After a better bridge was built between the town, Ragtown was officially renamed as (only slightly better) Iron Rod.

Silver Star's 250 residents enjoyed, by 1872, a hotel and several stores, and a Masonic and a "temperance" lodge. Men were employed in four mills and the mines. Not until the late 1880s did Whitehall—served by the Northern Pacific Railroad since 1883—surpass it as an area service center. But having rail transport nearby also sparked Silver Star's economy. High-grade ore lasted until around 1910, and some mines continued running into the 1930s. During the World War II federal shutdown of nonessential mines, a small chrome mine near town employed twenty men who dug 200 tons of chromite ore per day.

Estimates of Silver Star area precious metal production range from $2.5 million to $7 million.

Above: Silver Star's Broadway Mine.

Above left: Silver Star.
MONTANA HISTORICAL SOCIETY

Bottom left: The Broadway Mine.

Bottom right: Headframe at Rochester rises above a shaft nearly filled with water.

Facing page: Two views of Rochester.

AT THE SOUTHERN END OF THE Highland Mountains, west of the Jefferson River, Rochester failed as a placer camp because it had too little of the necessary water. But lode mining was possible. Within three years after the first gold was found on Watseca Hill in 1866, eight hundred men had rushed here, but underground mining of the Watseca Lode (found in 1869) is what kept the area alive. Then the mine's free-milling gold was gone in only two years, and digging had reached water level, requiring the expense of pumps to keep the mine open.

The 1872 Mining Law changed things by defining a claim in a way more appropriate to lode than to placer mining and thus protecting investors. With that legal encouragement, capitalists opened three new mines near the Watseca in 1873, and they were followed by several others from the 1880s to the 1910s. The Watseca continued to operate until 1980, like the entire district a steady but not stunning producer. Most other mines had closed by the end of the 1930s.

…The young man who carries the mail between Warm Springs creek and Highland, met with a severe accident…[H]e was driving a horse, attached to a sulky and…the horse commenced kicking furiously, breaking the young man's leg. He proceeded a short distance further, when the horse laid down, breaking the shafts…and pitching him to the ground, where he was compelled to remain for about three hours. A man passing, discovered his situation and took him immediately to [a nearby dwelling]. Dr. Beals [G.W. Beal] of German Gulch, was sent for, who came and set the broken limb. He is now quite comfortable, and doing as well as could be expected.

(Deer Lodge) *Weekly Independent*, Oct. 24, 1868

A Highland City resident foretold a bright future for his camp:

Many new buildings are in process of erection, and many more are in contemplation. Before the ides of November, we shall stand foremost among the bullion producing sections of the Territory.…

(Virginia City) *Montana Post*, March 9, 1867

And, in no time at all, a higher level of civilization arrived:

Professor McKibben has opened an Academy where he proposes educating the feet of the belles and beaux of the burg. His assemblies are well attended and give general satisfaction.

(Virginia City) *Montana Post*, March 30, 1867

…Times are very lively in Highland; merchants and business men generally, doing a good business. The three arrastras in the vicinity are all doing first rate.

(Virginia City) *Montana Post*, Aug. 14, 1868

A correspondent from Highland Gulch sent out this plea from the "new diggings" there:

Our quartz leads here are not to be beaten in the country. Out of a piece of rock no larger than a hazle-nut, we have obtained one grain and a half of pure silver; and there are two gold leads that you can wash out one hundred colors to the pan…

I hope, Mr. Editor, that you will not forget to put a paragraph in your valuable paper concerning this gulch. It would help us a great deal, as we have no store in the place, at present, and all that have their claims opened have plenty of money.

(Virginia City) *Montana Post*, Sept. 8, 1866

Progress continued in Highland City:

The weather has at last moderated and on every hand the pick of the miner can be heard, delving after the "filthy stuff," and the mechanics are driven to their utmost to complete warehouses, saloons, etc., in time for the season's trade. Our town presents a fine appearance. The major part of the evidence being handsome and imposing structures….Roberts, of the Exchange, had refitted and built an addition to his house, and is now to feed the hungry and rest the weary, in the best of style.

(Virginia City) *Montana Post*, April 6, 1867

Parrot

Down the Jefferson River and south of Whitehall stand the ruins of a large smelter that cost several million dollars and never processed even an ounce of ore. Weighing a thousand tons, it was moved from Butte to a hillside overlooking the river in 1895. The Parrot Smelter's Butte location hadn't supplied the needed amount of water, but here it could draw from Jefferson River water arriving via an eighteen-mile ditch from Silver Star.

Five hundred men were to be employed at the Parrot, and the company town around it was named Gaylord after Jared Gaylord, its superintendent, but people decided to call the whole place "Parrot." But, before the Parrot cranked up, Butte's Amalgamated Copper Company was created, and instantly owned a majority share of Parrot Mining Company stock. Of course, Amalgamated sent the ore to its Anaconda smelter, sold off what Parrot machinery it could, and left the building to fade away.

Above: The Parrot Smelter.

Below: Part of a cement works created for building the smelter.

MADISON RIVER & TOBACCO ROOT MOUNTAINS

MADISON RIVER &
TOBACCO ROOT MOUNTAINS

STERLING
MIDASBURG
RICHMOND FLATS
RED BLUFF
PONY

Sterling...is a small town depending upon Quartz alone for its existence and prosperity. There are several fine quartz mills at Sterling...

(Deer Lodge)
Weekly Independent
March 6, 1869

Quartz deposits protected the Tobacco Roots' silver and gold, and hard rock mining started early in the area. Mills popped up to refine the ore. Shift workers don't carry on the same way that gold rushers do, and soon the wild times of frontier days were fading.

Above: Pony's first quartz mill was built in 1876.
MONTANA HISTORICAL SOCIETY

Below: The Sterling Mill.

Sterling, Midasburg, Richmond Flats, Red Bluff

The ten gents who began the town of Sterling (near today's Norris) were hardy souls: They lived in dugouts through the winter of 1864–1865 while poking into the area's quartz for gold. Sterling became home to as many as 600 miners and their families, and its location made it the main stop on the Virginia City to Bozeman stagecoach route. Four quartz mills stood here, and the low-grade ore gave up about $9 to $12 per ton in gold. But the gold began to fade early in the 1870s, the miners moved on to the area's next big find, and the Sterling townsite was part of a farm by the 1880s.

…Life in all its multiple forms is manifesting itself quite significantly in and around Sterling at present. A large number of buildings of every shape and size, for store houses and residences, are being erected in every direction, so that there is not the slightest doubt that in a year hence Sterling will rank among the first towns in the Territory.

(Virginia City)
Montana Post
Nov. 9, 1867

ONLY 200 YARDS FROM STERLING WAS Midasburg, site of the Midas Company's mine and mill that employed ninety men. Neither little burg ever even had a post office.

THE DISTRICT'S STAR MINES WERE AT Richmond Flats, seven miles from Norris. Alex Norris, who had come to Sterling as an eighteen-year-old in 1864, founded the Revenue Mine in 1881. Perhaps having seen enough of failed mines during his years in the area, he sold the mine to Utah investors for the certain profit of $10,000 and got the heck out of the chancy mining business. Buying land, he started a cattle ranch and did quite well. The Revenue Mine yielded $2 million in gold until it was closed in 1921, but Alex Norris got a town named after him. The mine so overshadowed its setting that sometimes people called Richmond Flats "Revenue Flats."

Right next door to the rich Revenue Mine was the equally outstanding Monitor. The story, according to the Madison County Historical Association, tells of two miners hired to dig a tunnel, grub-staked for the winter, and sent to work. Unfortunately, they were digging parallel

Left: Midasburg stamp mill.

Below: Horseless rig, Midasburg.

Center: Midasburg, home to hard rock miners.

Above: Midasburg.

Left: Monitor Mine at Richmond Flats.

to what would be the Monitor's main vein. Nature gave them a hand one day while they took a lunch break outside in the sun. A cave-in exposed the four-foot-wide Monitor vein, which turned out to hold $6,000 of gold per ton when the price of gold was $19 an ounce.

Both the Monitor and the Revenue mines were working the same precious deposit, though, and the side-by-side mines were shut down for two years while the owners went to court to sort out who could follow which lead. The mines reopened as one company in 1900, and continued to produce until 1921. The Revenue alone was reopened and mined from 1936 to 1942.

EAST OF NORRIS, THE TOWN OF RED Bluff began after a prospector recorded only as Smith sank the first shaft into the quartz in 1864. His Red Bluff mine, mill, and boarding house gave their name to the camp where nine other mines were

Above: Red Bluff in 1895.
MONTANA HISTORICAL SOCIETY

Below: Red Bluff's hotel, which can be seen right of center in above bird's-eye picture.

The *Montana Post*'s Helena correspondent noted this demand to conform to his city's morals in August 1865:

A nymph of the pave, lately arrived from the northern mines, and consequently not well posted on the "customs of Montana," was enjoying the blessings of matrimony without the necessary legal qualification[.] The U.S. Grand Jury being in session, the erring fair and her dearly beloved were informed that an indictment would be found against them…and that the only path of safety led through the gates of matrimony. A "J.P." was sent for post haste, and the knot tied with the tongue, which, on better information, the lady would willingly have untied, but could not, even with her teeth.…

When a different county tried the same technique a few years later, things didn't turn out too well.

MURDER AT STERLING.—A man named Frank Hanna, formerly a ranchman on the Jefferson; last autumn a miner near Virginia [City], and recently a saloon keeper in Sterling, was murdered in that place…Hanna lived here last fall with a Hurdy Gurdy woman, known as "Black Hat," or "Black and Tan." The Grand Jury indicted them in the last session, and to avoid prosecution they…were married.…about six weeks ago.…On Tuesday night a man came into the saloon who we are informed had formerly been a husband or paramour of "Black Hat's," and swore "he had killed the —— and had a notion to go back and put another load into him." The men who were present went immediately to Hanna's cabin and found him shot and in a dying condition. He expired shortly after their arrival. The man was arrested…

(Virginia City) *Montana Post*, Nov. 11, 1868

When Deputy Sheriff Fish brought in George Hadzer for the Hanna murder on January 7, and Hadzer was "examined" in court, it was learned that Black Hat had been in "a condition of drunkenness at the time…that rendered her gloriously oblivious to all sublunary affairs." In court, she tagged two other men before identifying Hadzer as the killer.

Left: Morris-Elling Stamp Mill at Pony, with Hollowtop Mountain on the horizon.

Below: On Norwegian Creek southeast of Pony, dredge buckets survive.

I spent [a] day in visiting the mines and mills of the upper Hot Springs district [Sterling area], and there, as everywhere else in Montana, I was bewildered with the profusion of mineral wealth. The time for its systematic and successful development seems not yet at hand, but it cannot be long delayed. The interests of capital and miners need only to be harmonized, to give a very high measure of success to both....

A.K. McClure,
New York Tribune,
quoted in
(Virginia City)
Montana Post
Oct. 12, 1867

located by 1867. One of them, the Grub Stake, held its gold until 1877 before operators Pope, McKee, and Bayliss struck ore worth $60 to $80 per ton. The town was served by a general store with post office, a shoemaker, a blacksmith, a saloon, and a hotel. But things soured in 1890, when a railroad line reached nearby Norris, and the Red Bluff mine tunnels hit water in the shafts of low-grade ore. A brief renaissance occurred for the Red Bluff Mine in the first couple years of the 1900s. In the 1930s, the mine was drained, inspected, and left to fill again with water. Later, Red Bluff town buildings began to be used by a university agricultural experiment station. After the price of gold went up in the

1930s, the Grub Stake was reopened and was profitable until closure in 1942.

Pony

As the story goes, the town of Pony wasn't named for the creature, but rather for Smith McCumpsey—or maybe his name was Pony Smith or even Tecumseh Smith—who carried that nickname because of his compact stature. He found the first placer gold here on the east side of the Tobacco Root Mountains in 1867, and a brief-lived mining camp was called Pony Gulch. Quartz mining began in the

Above: Residents of Pony visiting relatives in Livingston created this tableau vivant for the camera. Fashionable in the late 19th century, tableaux vivantes (French for "living pictures") meant just that—real people freezing in position, usually to recreate a historical event or a work of art.
MONTANA HISTORICAL SOCIETY

Left: Morris State Bank, Pony.

Right: This unusually intact dredge survives in the central Madison River Valley.

Below: A dredge at work near Pony. The gravel-grabbing buckets moved through the superstructure on the left side.
MONTANA HISTORICAL SOCIETY

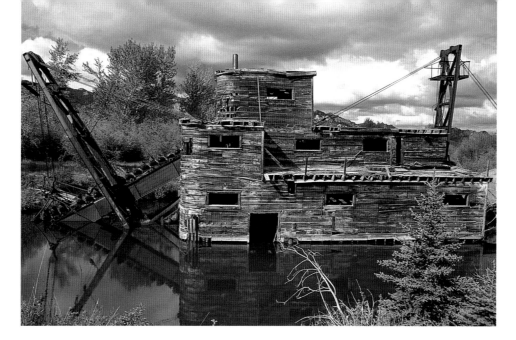

Above: A battery of ore-crushing stamps from a Pony stamp mill.

Right: Brothers and a new sled in front of the R. T. Smith home, Pony.

Crevice Mine seven years later, with its own mill opening as the area's first during the winter of 1875–1876.

The second and current site of still-alive-and-kicking Pony, between Pony and Willow creeks, was platted in 1876. Within sixteen months it boasted 250 residents in eighty homes, a post office, three hotels and three saloons, a butcher shop, two blacksmith shops, and two livery stables. School classes and church services were held in the same storefront. When word arrived about new gold strikes, Pony quickly lost population, but lode mining continued through the

1880s. Six nearby quartz mills and a sawmill employed some of the men, with more mills to be built over the years.

In 1890, the Northern Pacific Railroad opened a spur line into Pony. Decreased shipping costs meant that lower-grade ore was worth sending to smelters in Butte, Anaconda, and East Helena. Mining continued into the 1930s, when the increased price of gold again livened up life for the 1,000 residents. By then, Pony's Mineral Hill Mining District had given up $6.4 million, mostly in gold but with notable amounts of silver, copper, and lead.

The Eastern mail arrives semi-occasionally. Cause—snow blockade on the Union Pacific. It appears that the only future reliance the people of Montana have in the prompt delivery of mails is the completion of the Northern Pacific Railroad.

(Deer Lodge)
Weekly Independent
Feb. 3, 1872

LEWIS AND CLARK RANGE

There is a fair prospect of our camp [in Lincoln Gulch] being overstocked with traders, saloon keepers and fancy women—all after the "loose change" of the honest miner.

letter to (Deer Lodge)
Weekly Independent
April 24, 1868

The Lewis and Clark Range, main range of the Rocky Mountains, passes west of Helena, with mines spread along both sides of the range and its spine, the Continental Divide. Development began on the west side, as miners moved away from the original gold strikes in the 1860s, and then moved to the east side toward the Missouri River, then finally up onto the spine itself in the 1880s.

Above: Marysville in its prime, as photographed by William Hall.
MONTANA HISTORICAL SOCIETY

Below: Blackfoot City.

Blackfoot City, Marysville, Bald Butte, Rimini

Lying between today's Avon and Marysville, Ophir Gulch was one of two sites (the other was downstream from Fort Benton on the Missouri River) named by early miners in reference to a fabled source of gold mentioned in the Old Testament. Those first placer miners came into the

area in May 1865, and placered in Ophir and such colorfully named nearby gulches as Deadwood, Snowshoe, Eureka, and Tiger, as well as the mundane-sounding Carpenter. In 1865, Deadwood Gulch gave up the largest gold nugget ever found in Montana, then worth $3,280.

Miners named the central town Blackfoot City. It had two long parallel streets and a few short cross streets lined with

Right: Blackfoot City in 1865.
MONTANA HISTORICAL SOCIETY

cabins, with businesses on one of the long streets. When the New York *Tribune's* A.K. McClure came by in 1867, he noted that "[h]alf the cabins are groggeries, about one-fifth are gambling saloons, and a large percentage are occupied by the fair but frail ones who ever follow the miner's camp." But there were also two doctors, seven mercantiles, and a carpenter who also built the coffins carried up to the cemetery on Butcher Ridge south of town.

Blackfoot City burned down in June 1869, but was rebuilt. Its peak population was around 1,500, including a considerable number of Chinese by the 1870s; one of the Chinese merchants obtained fireworks from his homeland for the town's celebration of the United States' centennial in 1876. When Blackfoot City burned down again in 1882, the rebuilt settlement was given the name Ophir. By then, an estimated 500 Chinese men worked in the underground mines, and Ophir had a section called Chinatown. After an estimated $3.5 million in placer gold was

obtained from the district, lode mining continued into the 1880s, and dredging filled the creeks with its telltale tailings piles in the mid-1930s.

MARYSVILLE'S PLACER GOLD WAS FIRST found in Silver Creek in 1862, but richer ore came out of the creek's gravel bars beginning in 1864. The only known record from before 1880 shows that $50,000 in placer gold came out of them in 1869 alone. Miners named their camp after an early resident, Mrs. Mary Ralston. The town, which once boasted 5,000 residents and its own railroad

spur line, continues today on a much smaller scale, mixing contemporary homes with restored old homes and abandoned buildings.

The district's biggest success story is that of Thomas Cruse, known as "Tommy," an immigrant who relocated an abandoned claim in 1876 and named it Drumlummon after his birth parish in Ireland. Perhaps the earlier claimant had given up on the site, but Cruse didn't, and he kept digging all alone even when he had to borrow money to pay his taxes. Eventually he struck rich ore, and recovered $144,539

Above and right: Marysville.

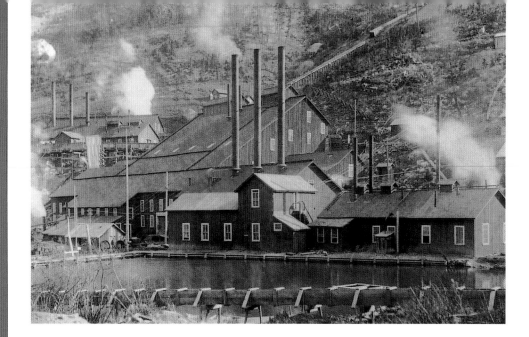

Left: *Marysville's Drumlummon mine and mill.*
MONTANA HISTORICAL SOCIETY

Below: *Up the mountain, at Bald Butte.*

Bottom left: *Bald Butte.*

Bottom right: *Methodist Episcopal church, Marysville.*

in bullion. In 1880, he built a five-stamp mill near the mine.

Three years later, the astute Cruse sold the Drumlummon mine and mill to an English corporation for $1 million in cash and another half million in stock. Cruse built a brick mansion in Helena, bought a coach-and-four and hired a driver, and started small banks in both Helena and Marysville. He guaranteed building of the state capitol by buying up its unsold bonds, and donated the land and funds for building the Cathedral of St. Helena. At age fifty, he married the daughter of future

U.S. Senator Thomas Carter, but she died in childbirth only a year later. After losing his wife, Cruse became unhappy with the new way of life. He took to hanging out by the mine adits in Marysville, and later found satisfaction by buying the Bald Mountain Mine on Bald Butte above town.

The Drumlummon's new owners built a fifty-stamp, and then a sixty-stamp mill, in 1884 and 1886. Miners were now digging lower-quality ore, but even worse, in 1889 they crossed the boundary between the Drumlummon and adjoining St. Louis Mining

Company property. Drumlummon miners fired up stink pots to drive back St. Louis miners, who in turn built a bulkhead to keep out the Drumlummon men. The lawsuit that St. Louis brought in 1892 lasted until 1910, when it was decided in favor of St. Louis Mining. During the suit, far less mining was done in the Drumlummon. St. Louis Mining bought the Drumlummon in 1911 and worked it until 1948. The vast mill burned down in the 1970s.

Tommy Cruse's "hobby" mine, the Bald Mountain at the head of Dog Creek, started producing in 1882. It flourished from 1890 to 1901 when rich ore was found and a twenty-stamp mill (soon expanded to forty stamps), and again from the late 1910s to 1923, and

Above: Bald Mountain Mine cable hoist was driven by a Model T engine.

Top: Bald Mountain Mill, above Marysville.
MONTANA HISTORICAL SOCIETY

Below: Bald Mountain Mine's generator building.

One of the claims in Basin creek turned out this week, one hundred and seven ounces of gold, from eight days run. This is encouraging, and should have the effect of making men do more prospecting in the future. There are hundreds of bars and gulches scattered around that only awaits the pick and shovel of the hardy miner [t]o unearth their auriferous wealth. No use of lounging around; fortunes are to be made in Montana, but they must be worked out with untiring industry until success is achieved.

(Maiden) *Mineral Argus*, July 31, 1884

The Wickes…smelting works are treating about 160 tons of ore daily.

Mining Review, quoted in (Maiden) *Mineral Argus*, May 15, 1884

The town of Blackfoot is just now en dishabille—changing her somber and somewhat seedy garb for a light and airy summer dress…Business, too, is now brisk; strange faces predominate; pack-trains come and go; merchandise (particularly whisky) has a downward tendency, and the people are happy…

(Virginia City) *Montana Post*, April 10, 1866

A letter from Blackfoot City reports some, but not enough, progress:

…Notwithstanding the great wickedness of this people, yet they have been looked upon with favor, perhaps on account of the few faithful ones who live here; but be that as it may, we have a post office. However, it has not yet been any benefit to us, as no mail key has arrived for use of the office. That it may soon come is the earnest prayer of all.…

(Virginia City) *Montana Post*, July 14, 1866

Left: Some Rimini dwellings serve today as summer and even year-round homes.

Below: Rimini.

Bottom: Rimini community center.

Bottom left: Driver Joseph Bierman poses in the Rimini Stage in front of the Red Mountain Hotel, Rimini, in 1908.

MONTANA HISTORICAL SOCIETY

then from 1931 to 1942. Records available for 1902 to 1942 show that during those years Bald Mountain Mine produced 55,390.9 ounces of gold, 49,020 ounces of silver, 34,814 pounds of copper, and 290,509 pounds of lead.

RIMINI, JUST EAST AND DOWNHILL from the Continental Divide, sits in the narrow Ten Mile Creek valley between towering Red Mountain on its east and Lee Mountain on its west. Rimini served about one hundred mines in the surrounding mountains, where silver lode mining began in 1864 but flourished in the 1880s. By then, rail con-

nections took the ore to Wickes for processing, and later to East Helena. Lower silver prices slowed but didn't stop mining in the 1890s, and by 1958 the Rimini Mining District had produced close to $10 million in silver, gold, copper, and lead.

Like Marysville, Rimini has both ghost and living sections, especially summer homes. One of its colorful uses was as a training camp for military dog-sled mushers during World War II. With Allied bombers flying over the northern transpolar route, these men rescued military flight crews downed in extreme snow-and-ice conditions.

Basin, Wickes, Corbin, Comet

Cataract and Basin creeks flow down from the Lewis and Clark Range to meet the Boulder River half a mile apart. Placer miners found good but not great gold in Cataract Creek in 1862, but when they heard of the Grasshopper Creek (Bannack) strike, they left. Granville and James Stuart and Reece Anderson, their strike at Gold Creek four years behind them, soon built cabins at the mouth of Cataract Creek and tried their hands here. Another camp at the mouth of Basin Creek drew Cataract's residents, who even moved their buildings.

In 1880, the camp at Basin Creek named itself Basin City, became the service center for the area, and grew to a population of 1,500 over the next twenty-five years. During those years, several mines developed silver-lead lodes. The major gold mines, the Katy and the Hope, opened in the early 1890s. They were reorganized under the Basin and Bay State Mining Company in 1894, and production continued at a lesser level until around 1911. Basin's population fell off. In 1924, the Katy-Hope (now physically joined underground), and White Ele-

phant mines were reopened under the Jib Consolidated Mining Company. For the two years they turned out gold ore worth $1.7 million, Basin's population went up again. Then shady stock dealings shut down the Jib operation, permanently.

Today, the surviving portion of Basin is a small community of individualists, including a number of artists and musicians.

NORTHWEST OF BASIN, A CLUSTER OF lode mines led to creation of the once-premier smelting town of Wickes, some of which was destroyed by wildfire in the summer of 2000, ninety-eight years after fire first took most of its buildings.

From 1883 until 1893, Montana (Territory, then State in 1889) was the nation's second-largest silver producer, and Wickes—settled in 1877—was the center of one of Montana's richest silver areas. Records covering 1883 to 1900 show that this district gave up $50 million worth of silver and other metals.

The Gregory and Minah lodes were located in 1864, the Alta in 1869, and the Comet in 1874, but lode mining didn't flourish until the 1880s. The Gregory Mine had had Montana Territory's second smelter, built in 1867, but it was of low efficiency. The Helena and Livingston Smelting & Reduction Company's Alta

Top: Basin on fire in November 1903.
MONTANA HISTORICAL SOCIETY

Top left: Basin's hoosegow.

Above center: Wickes Mine and Smelter crew around 1899; boys were employed to crawl into tight spaces too small for grown men.
MONTANA HISTORICAL SOCIETY

Above: Mine tailings, Wickes.

The railroad spur came into Elkhorn on a 125-foot-high trestle, and Sheriff John William later recalled that "at one point across the canyon it made a horseshoe turn" that he thought probably thrilled child passengers more than modern airplane rides.

Mine, one mile from Wickes, had had its own smelter, but that burned down. Finally, in 1883, Gregory Mine owner Seligman and Helena Mining & Reduction Company owner Samuel T. Hauser persuaded the brand-new Northern Pacific Railroad to lay a line to the area. Later, the Great Northern put its line through here also. When cheaper shipping was promised, Hauser rebuilt the smelter as the largest of its type in Montana, and added a concentrator for Comet Mine ore.

Wickes was named for an Alta Mine engineer, W. W. Wickes. During the town's boom years from 1883 to 1893,

the homes and businesses of up to 1,500 residents spread for a mile and a half along the gulch. Four hundred and fifty men worked in the mines and mills. Ten kilns made 25,000 bushels of charcoal a month to keep its large smelter going, and ore came from around western Montana and northern Idaho for processing.

The International Order of Good Templars lodge building arose in 1880, and the Presbyterian church in 1882. A dozen and a half saloons served miners, mill workers, and railroad crews. The five dance halls ran day as well as night to accommodate miners' work schedules.

Above left: The Alta Mine at Wickes.
MONTANA HISTORICAL SOCIETY

Above: Last of the original three smelter stacks at Wickes.

Below: Corbin.

Below left: The mill built during Comet's second boom, of the 1920s and 1930s.

The smelter closed with the end of the Silver Purchase Act, and Alta Mine ore went to East Helena for smelting until 1896. Northern Pacific closed the railroad line to Helena in 1900.

WHEN HELENA MINING & REDUCTION Company went on its building binge in 1883, it had built a concentrator for the Alta Mine on flat land at a camp called Corbin, where a few cabins and frame buildings would stand. Two later concentrators, one in 1896 and one in 1925, were built to reprocess Alta tailings, the second running 1938–1941.

Right: The Comet Mine.

Above: Mine elevator cage at Comet.

Above right: Comet.

SOUTHWEST OF WICKES, THE COMET Mine's rich lode had been located in 1874, but was not developed until Alta Mine's owners did so in 1883. At first, ore went by wagon to the Wickes smelter, then the following year a rope tramway began carrying it between the mine and Wickes. Perhaps 300 people lived in Comet at its peak in the 1880s, but it was empty by World War I. The mine opened again in the 1920s in the 1930s, and a mill was built in 1926; during this second boom, 300 men were employed in the two operations, and the town was said to hold twenty-

two saloons. The mill was sold for salvage in 1941, and the mine has been worked on a small scale off and on since the end of World War II.

Radersburg, Hassel (St. Louis)

Crow Creek's placer gravel was first worked in 1866, and locals say that from then until 1906, at least half a million dollars in loose gold came out of the creek. Looking for the source of the gold led two of the first-year prospec-

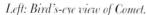

On January 2, 1892,
the *Helena Independent*
reported that bullion
from the Holter mine at
Elkhorn for the week
ending November 28,
1891, had been worth
$8,450, from ore that
held 86 ounces of silver
per ton. During the year,
the Holter mine had paid
$475,000 in dividends to
its stockholders.

Left: Bird's-eye view of Comet.

*Below: International Order of the Odd Fellows
lodge, Radersburg.*

tors, John Keating and David Blacker,
up into the hills to the district's richest
mine, the Keating. Working the free-
milling gold with a simple arrastra, the
partners made $40,000 to $50,000 during each of the next four years. In 1870,
a fifteen-stamp mill was erected, soon
joined by four smaller mills. Four other
mines were developed.

The lodes were good, but placer gold
in Crow Creek, and plenty of water
coming down from the mountains to
work it, was the area's making. Sluicing
and hydraulicking took over. A farmer
named Reuben Rader donated land for

a townsite, which was named in his
honor and laid out with two streets
named simply Front and Back. The
International Order of Good Templars
built a two-story frame lodge.

From the beginning, Radersburg had
many families with more women (of
the honorable type) than most mining
camps of 600 residents. Their home-
making lives couldn't have been easy:
during winter, water had to be purchased from a man who hauled it from
Crow Creek. The butcher shop stood
near the slaughterhouse and livery stable, with mosquito netting the only pro-

tection for its wares. The first log
school house's dirt roof sifted silt down
onto pupils' clothing.

The town supported fourteen
saloons during its heyday. Although it
had been the seat of Jefferson County,
with the required courthouse and jail,
Radersburg lost the honor to Boulder
in 1883, three years after its population
plummeted from 250 to only sixty-nine.

But one honor the village still holds
came in 1905. Mrs. Della Johnston
Williams of Helena happened to be visiting her parents' home in Radersburg
when daughter Myrna decided to be

Above: At the edge of Radersburg.

*Left: Although the Denver was in Nevada City,
residents of Radersburg and all the new camps
were treated to fresh meat stored this way.*

MONTANA HISTORICAL SOCIETY

Right: Hassel.

Below: Radersburg.

Center: Side-street businesses at Radersburg.

Bottom: Keating Mines headframe near Radersburg.

Right: Looking across Hassel to Copper Hill.

COURTESY OF VIVIAN McMURRY

born. As a little girl in Helena, Myrna would sometimes play with a neighbor boy, Judge Cooper's son Frank. When they went to work in motion pictures, she took the stage name Myrna Loy, and for his stage name he changed Frank to Gary.

BACK WHEN CROW CREEK GOLD HAD been found in 1866, placer gold was discovered up nearby Indian Creek, eight miles from future Radersburg. The season when water was available for placering was short, but miners soon began simple quartz mining, with shallow tunnels and open pits. Chinese miners were reported to be digging the Ten Mile Tunnel in bedrock under Indian Creek's prehistoric channel. The log-cabin settlement that began in 1875 with forty or so miners was called St. Louis until the 1890s, when it was renamed to honor pioneer miner Joseph E. Hassel. Joe Hassel had lived comfortably from his solo mining, but not grandly. Three small stamp mills processed ore from the area.

When the town was christened Hassel, it had several businesses, a Masonic lodge, and some frame homes. Hassel

Left: Some of the Diamond Hill Mill's 120 stamps, at Hassel.
COURTESY OF VIVIAN McMURRY

Below: A Hassel ore chute.

Center: Diamond Hill Mill.
COURTESY OF VIVIAN McMURRY

Bottom: Hassel.

BLACKFOOT CITY
is still the small, thrifty, enterprising, well watered mining town it was last spring, and has not, like many of her sister hamlets of the Territory, retrograded....A few, of course, after a successful summer's work, have taken their homeward flight, others are ready to go, while new comers are arriving daily, from the adjacent small gulches to winter.

(Virginia City)
Montana Post
Sept. 28, 1867

Miners' Union, affiliated with the Western Federation of Miners, organized in 1895.

"Capitalists" (investors) developed deeper mines on nearby Diamond Hill and Giant Hill in the late 1870s, mines worked until the early 1900s. A 120-stamp mill went to work in 1895 to treat ore from several mines on Diamond Hill.

Area mining pretty much shut down by 1910, then reopened from the mid-1930s until the World War II closure. Dredging that began on Indian Creek in 1946 destroyed mine tunnels, altered the creek, and covered most of Hassel with high waste piles.

Copper City

South of Radersburg and six miles north of Three Forks, Copper City's story is one of many false starts and few profitable moments.

Gold was found in the area in 1864, but getting equipment to the remote site put things off until the 1870s. Four partners started a quartz mine, but the lead they followed disappeared.

In the 1880s, a bit of high grade quartz ore was found, and several claims were staked in the area, including a silver mine and an iron mine.

Left: Copper City.

Right, below, center, and bottom: Gould, including (below) the sealed mine shaft.

Gould

The Jay Gould Mine, primary producer among about a dozen mines in this district atop the Continental Divide northwest of Helena, was worked from 1884 to 1890, its high-grade ore processed in a ten-stamp mill. Its heydays were 1903–1907 (with 150 men underground) and 1910–1914 (with only 40 miners). Up to 1915, gold from the Jay Gould was valued at $2.5 million; later intermittent working

added another half million to the total.

The mine apparently was named after a nationally known financier who had nothing to do with it. Jay Gould's notorious claim to fame was that he and another, James Fisk, had almost succeeded in cornering the United States gold market in 1869. Learning just in time that the federal government was going to step in, they quickly sold off their gold, which set off the Panic of 1869 but left them rich. By the time the Jay Gould Mine sought to "corner the gold market," its namesake was busy manipulating railroad stock.

Right: The Jay Gould Mine in its prime.
MONTANA HISTORICAL SOCIETY

In 1954, Boulder resident Charles R. W. Warren, then 78, reminisced to the *Montana Standard* that

We used to go to Elkhorn for dances at Fraternity Hall. Always had a good time up there. Seems like that town had more getup than most places.

Elkhorn's relative accessibility makes it one of Montana's most-visited ghost towns, its surviving buildings clustered in the gulch that once hummed with railway cars, and its poignant small cemetery asleep up a steep hill. Fraternity Hall, high on the state's most-photographed-buildings list, represents 19th century can-do community spirit at its best.

Above: Elkhorn in 1913.
UNIVERSITY OF MONTANA LIBRARY

Below: A false-fronted source of Elkhorn libations.

Elkhorn

Fraternity Hall in Elkhorn is one of Montana's most famous ghost town survivors, and so it *should* be. Residents of this silver mining town created and used the building as a community social club, and they opened it right at the end of Western silver prosperity.

Swiss immigrant Peter Wys died two years after locating his claim in 1870, the first in this small gulch within the Elkhorn Mountains. Anton M. Holter's Elkhorn Mining Company began to develop Wys's claim in 1875, within six years reaching the 300-foot level. First known as the Holter Mine, it was later called the Elkhorn. In 1883, a new incarnation of the company built a ten-stamp mill, which they enlarged to

Right: Elkhorn.

Below: Locals say that Italians were required to live in Dagotown, north of Elkhorn.

Bottom: Victims of the diphtheria epidemic.

twenty and then twenty-five stamps. When poorer ore showed up at the 800-foot level, the Montana owners sold to a British corporation in 1888 for half a million dollars.

Using the same corporate name, the new owners improved the mill and developed new leads underground, within two years paying owners dividends worth more than the purchase price.

In 1887, a Northern Pacific Railroad spur line from Boulder was completed into Elkhorn, the daily train rumbling into town on its thrilling trestle loaded with supplies and luxuries, and leaving with silver ore. But 500 woodcutting jobs ended when the railroad was complete, and those men and their families moved on. The town's population peak of 1,500 to 2,500 was permanently past.

Elkhorn's saddest tale is recorded in its tiny cemetery, up a steep hill from town. In 1889, a diphtheria epidemic took the lives of many children and some of their mothers. Gravestones record the deaths of child after child within the same family, sometimes only days apart.

During the silver boom of the 1880s, Elkhorn was a lively but usually mannerly town. Men attended lodge meetings, public dances were frequent, and residents could relax at the two-lane bowling alley. In the summer, there were miners' drilling contests, baseball games, and horse races.

Sloping down the gulch, Main Street boasted saloons, three hotels, the Elkhorn Trading Company and other mercantiles, and shops for the candy-maker, butcher, jeweler, and barber; from 1884 to 1924, there was also a post office. A livery stable and an ice house provided their essential services, and woodcutters and water wagons made daily deliveries to housewives. A doctor served the public and also contracted as

Prices kept pace with miners' earnings, as August 1865 costs from Diamond City, Montana Territory show. The men were making $20 to $50 a day, about $222 to $555 in today's dollars. A hundred-pound bag of flour cost $30 (equal to $333 today), a pound of bacon was 70¢ ($7.77) and ham was 75¢ ($8.33). The picks and shovels essential to their work cost from $10 to $15 and $8 to $10 respectively, equivalent to $111 to $166 and $88 to $111.

At the beginning of that December, flour had gone up to $36 ($400) per bag, but at least that was better than late the first winter of Alder Gulch's strike, when it had reached $100 ($1,100). The latter caused a riot, with miners breaking into stores to take flour until the Vigilantes put a halt to it by threatening to shoot any thief. The Vigilance Committee repaid storeowners (most of whom were Vigilantes) for the lost flour.

company physician with one of the area's lesser mines. Methodists were the only churchgoers to erect their own building.

What was needed, residents decided, was a social center. They raised money—a community talent show was one project—and built Fraternity Hall on Main Street. Different lodge groups took turns using the second floor for their secret meetings, but everyone shared the large room and smaller reception hall downstairs. The big room's raised stage hosted bands playing for many dances and parties, and also served troupes of traveling actors and lecturers. The local Cornish Glee Club and the Elkhorn Brass Band performed at the grand opening on the Fourth of July, 1893.

On November 1 that same year, repeal of the Silver Purchase Act and immediate layoffs at some Elkhorn mines signaled the beginning of the end. Population was down to 600 by year's end, and the rail line and the Elkhorn Mine itself closed in 1900. Other owners mined and reworked tailings off and on in the early 1900s, again in 1922, 1937, 1943, and 1948, and for the final time in 1951.

Today one acre of Elkhorn's townsite is protected as a Montana state park, surrounded by private land and some homes and cabins still in use.

Right: The Kleinschmidt Mine.

Below: The Elkhorn Mine reduction works, around 1890.
MONTANA HISTORICAL SOCIETY

Above: The East Pacific Mine, near Winston.

Right: This flume once carried water out of Indian Creek Gulch.

Winston Area

A little gold, and much more silver and lead, from the East Pacific Mine above Spring Gulch on the northeastern slopes of the Elkhorns made Robert A. Bell a fortune. In 1896, he bought the mine and its adjoining mill from the Winston Brothers, who worked on contract for Northern Pacific Railroad as ore-haulers. Over the next dozen years, Bell prospered. He was smart enough to get out when the rich veins began to thin, but not smart enough to keep from losing his mining-business money in the brand-new Texas oil business.

Four more mines were opened as part of the East Pacific group, which produced $3 million in gold, two thirds of that from the four and a half miles of tunnels in the East Pacific Mine itself.

Two miles south, atop the Elkhorns, the Kleinschmidt was among eight small mines that dug into the same deposit of not-very-rich ore. The east-west veins held silver/lead, and north-south veins offered gold. In 1928, Montana-Idaho Mines Corporation began operating both the Kleinschmidt and the East Pacific group.

WEST CENTRAL
MONTANA

BARKER
HUGHESVILLE
NEIHART
MONARCH
CASTLE
ROBINSON
INDEPENDENCE MINE

WEST CENTRAL MONTANA

We learn…that Bob Bales, of Butte, has taken charge of the smelter at Barker, and is making a far better showing at less expense than was being done under the [previous] management. It is thought now that the smelter will run all summer. This will be a good turn for Barker if such is the case.

(Maiden)
Mineral Argus
May 29, 1884

A short time since a couple of thieves stole a span of mules from the smelter company at Barker. Sheriff Cameron traced them to Wicks [*sic*], effected a capture and landed them safely in jail at White Sulphur.

(Lewistown)
Mineral Argus
May 29, 1884

Silver and lead were the main treasures hidden in the hard rock of west-central Montana, where the boom time was brief, lasting from the 1880s until the bottom dropped out of the silver market in 1893. Now the mountains and gulches see more recreationists than miners, and the cabins that dot the landscape include many summer and weekend homes.

Above: Castle in 1888.
MONTANA HISTORICAL SOCIETY

Below: Barker.

LITTLE BELT MOUNTAINS

Barker, Hughesville, Neihart, Monarch

On Galena Creek in the Little Belt Mountains, E.A. "Buck" Barker and Patrick Hughes each had camps named after them after they spotted the area's

first silver ore in the autumn of 1879. Galena Creek and Barker were up the mountainside from Hughesville. Shallow mines in the district produced high-grade silver/lead ore with some gold during the 1880s. Barker and Hughes sold to investors who included Great Falls founder Paris Gibson and Great Falls businessman W. G. Conrad in the early 1890s. Senator Thomas Power bought

Right: Hughesville.

Below: A Barker adit.

Above: An especially grand log structure, Barker.

Right: Clendenin Smelter at Barker.

several claims, including the second one made by Barker and Hughes, and combined them in 1902 as his Block P Mine at Hughesville. He sold out in 1927, but the mine was worked off and on until 1943—as Montana's greatest lead mine after 1929. The Block P's ore was processed at a mill that Power built in 1910–1911 at Barker, where bunkhouses and a boarding house sheltered the miners.

SOUTHWEST OF BARKER AND HUGHESville, in the center of the Little Belts, prospectors spreading out from the early camps discovered the richness of the

Neihart district in July 1881, when the romantically named Queen of the Mountains Mine was claimed. This brought more miners and prospectors, lowering Barker's and Hughesville's populations. The town of Neihart—at first Canyon City, then renamed for an area resident who was one of the discoverers—formed in a narrow canyon on Belt Creek and the next year qualified for its own post office. A rough wagon road soon connected it to the town of White Sulphur Springs, but Neihart ore was packed by mule to Barker and Hughesville for processing

Left: *Neihart on July 25, 1888.*
MONTANA HISTORICAL SOCIETY

Below: *All the services are available at Neihart,
even town-lot sales for nearby Monarch.*
MONTANA HISTORICAL SOCIETY

at the Clendenin smelter until that
closed in 1883. The Neihart district got
its own concentrator and smelter at the
Mountain Chief Mine in 1885.

Neihart was a modest village of fifty
houses and many tents, served by the
post office, two each of saloons, restaurants, hotels, and horse stables, and a
blacksmith shop and a boarding house.
Its mining economy fell apart after 1893,
but Neihart survives to the present.

From 1882 until 1929, the Neihart
(originally Montana) Mining District
produced $16 million in silver.

Transportation costs depressed area

mining until 1891, when the Great
Northern Railroad built into the area. But
in only two years the silver market fell.
Fortune smiled again during and just
after World War I, and in 1929 and 1935.

MONARCH, A STOP ON THE RAILROAD
thirteen miles north of Neihart, built up
right along the tracks down in the
canyon bottom. In addition to the railroad station that once hummed with ore
shipments from the area and the post
office that opened in 1889 and continues
today, it boasted a school house, a
church, and a small shopping district.

Above middle: Neihart Cemetery.

Above and left: Neihart.

Right: Castle.

Below: Neihart.

Center and bottom: Castle.

Right: Castle.

CASTLE MOUNTAINS

Castle, Robinson

Separately, two experienced prospectors—Hanson Barnes in 1882 and F. L. "Lafe" Hensley in 1885—explored into the Castle Mountains and recognized their riches. The boom lasted only until 1893, but in those few years the town of Castle was home to 1,500 to 2,000 people. The few streets of its eighty-acre townsite were congested with freight wagons bringing in mining supplies and taking out ore.

Castle boasted a fine school house, a photo gallery, and a brass band in addition to its fourteen saloons and nine mercantiles. Male residents could attend meetings of the Castle Miners' Union, the Odd Fellows, or the Knights of Pythias, and women had an active chapter of the Women's Christian Temperance Union.

A mile from town, the Cumberland Mine was the district's largest and richest. At first using the Yellowstone Mine's smelter, then with its own opening in 1891, the Cumberland briefly was Montana's largest lead producer.

A terrible murder was committed at Clendenin, Barker district, a week ago…It seems that one, Murane, was suspected by Peter McDermott of being too attentive to his wife. McDermott accused him of it and the result of a conference on the subject seemed to be amicable to both parties. On the night of the killing McDermott sent for Murane and his sister to come to his house. Directly upon their arrival McDermott fired four shots into Murane's body, killing him instantly. The deed was committed in the presence of McDermott's wife and the sister of the deceased. The murdered man only said: "he gave me a poor show for my life." The murder[er] fled. He took no horse with him. It is supposed by some that the murderer committed suicide as he had threatened to do in a previous conversation with his wife. Up to the shooting McDermott had always borne a good reputation. At the inquest, Mrs. McDermott confessed her wrong-doing, but this is not credited by some.

(Maiden)
Mineral Argus
Aug. 21, 1884

An easily stored amount of gold dust had disproportionately high value, as a Virginia City merchant was reminded. On an autumn evening, it seems that not everyone was engrossed in the play onstage at the theater, because someone broke into I. H. Castor's store. The newspaper noted that "$1,408, in bankable dust was stolen out of the desk."

(Virginia City)
Montana Post
Sept. 16, 1865

The cost of freighting the ore out was horrendous, and new owners closed the mine in 1892 to await the Montana Railroad's promised arrival. The Panic of 1893 delayed Richard Harlow's building of the rail line, and the mine stayed closed. Harlow never did build all the way to Castle. The Cumberland was reopened in the 1940s, and again in 1957.

Nearby, George P. Robinson located the Top Mine in 1885, and Paul Grandy and N. A. Nelson jointly located two mines two years later. The camp around these properties was named Robinson, but during its short life didn't even reach a population of 300.

ABSAROKA MOUNTAINS

Independence Mine

At the very southern edge of west-central Montana—120 miles southeast of Neihart—the Independence Mining District lies in the Absaroka Mountains, which include Montana's highest peaks.

This land was part of the Crow Indian

Above: Independence.

Left: Robinson.

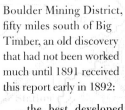

Right: Independence.

Above and right: Stamps left from some of Independence's seven mills.

Reservation until 1882, and early prospectors had been kicked out by the federal government. The boom here was from 1883 to 1893, and it centered on the town of Independence, south of today's Big Timber. Independence was the site of seven stamp mills, and became the district's small service center. Because of the mining activity, the town received electricity in 1893, but at the same time its remoteness required five days of horse-drawn travel to reach Big Timber.

Gold, silver, copper, and lead came out of Independence Mining District properties. Today's mining authorities state that district gold production was "much greater than" the modest $120,000 recorded from 1890 to 1905.

The Independence Mine itself produced not-too-rich ore during 1894–1897, 1900–1904, 1928, and 1931. In 1934, a Big Timber doctor leased and reopened the Independence until two miners were killed in an accident; it was then closed.

A revival was noted for the

…mining camp of San Martina…on Nine-Mile creek on the site of an old placer camp. Recent discoveries of quartz have attracted considerable attention… Several large veins of rich gold quartz have been discovered in this formation during the past year.

Helena Independent
Jan. 9, 1892

NORTHWESTERN & WESTERN MONTANA

The mountains and narrow valleys of Montana's northwestern edge are logging country now, but their days of golden glory extended into the 1930s at some locations. Placering for incredibly pure gold nuggets gave way to digging deep underground along gold veins buried in quartz rock. Eventually, profits went to out-of-state investors.

Above: The ore train and its mini-locomotive on their trestle at Pardee.
MONTANA HISTORICAL SOCIETY

Below: Cinkers Mine, Louisville.

Louisville, Pardee, and Keystone

Louis A. Barrette and his partner, B. Lanthier, French Canadian prospectors unhappy with pickings on the Idaho side of the Continental Divide, moved east to begin placering Cedar Creek in 1869. This area's placer gold was nearly pure, and over the next fifteen years, miners took out anywhere from $1 million to $10 million worth, depending on who told the tale.

Barrette and Lanthier managed to get $375 in gold over a few weeks in the fall, and staked out several claims for themselves. When winter set in and they needed supplies, though, they left to stay at another Frenchman's ranch on the Clark Fork. Somehow word of their strike got out and, in January 1870, the rush was on.

Right: Part of Pardee's red light district.

Below: Below: Cinkers Mine, Louisville.

Below center: Nozzle and pipes for hydraulic mining, at the Amador Mine.

Bottom: The Amador Mine.

Right: Iron Mountain Mine, Pardee.

Within two weeks, Louisville was the first camp built on land cleared of its thick forest. In addition to the usual mining accidents, men suffered injuries from falling trees or the axes used on them. Louisville immediately boasted twelve cabins, but it didn't become the district's main center. Camps popped up along Cedar Creek wherever another strike was made, and 800 people were in the area before the first chilly month ended. In 1870, there were 7,000 residents, but Cedar Creek was empty only four years later. After white miners abandoned Louisville, Chinese miners moved in to work the creek and rework the tailings, giving one area the name China Gulch.

Barrette got together a group of investors in 1884 and continued to take gold from Cedar Creek until 1906.

The Amador (later Gildersleeve) Mine opened in 1902, tunneling into hard rock under Cedar Creek. The district saw another spurt of mining activity in the 1930s.

NORTHEAST OF SUPERIOR, PARDEE came into being in 1888–1889, near the Amador, Keystone, and Iron Mountain mines. The latter—owned by James K.

A New York newspaper correspondent's description of the Montana gold camps, republished in the *Montana Post*, included this bit of "color."

The phrases of some of the miners are original and suggestive. They call the fine particles of gold in the earth "the color." One of them remarked of a man tried in various positions and found utterly worthless:

"I have panned him out, clear down to the bed rock, but I can't even raise the colors."

(Virginia City)
Montana Post
Nov. 10, 1866

$55 million was the mineral production value from Montana's "ranges and mines" in 1891, excluding coal.

Pardee—was this district's bellwether, and its closure in 1897 ended the employment of 100 to 125 miners. Pardee was soon mostly abandoned, its boarding house, Miners' Union Hall, saloon, dance halls and gambling parlors quiet. Then a fire took out most of the empty homes and businesses. The Iron Mountain Mine produced again from 1909 to 1930.

KEYSTONE IS THE THIRD AND FINAL name for a town on Keystone Creek near the St. Regis Bend of the Clark Fork River. It began as O'Rourke, after Phillip O'Rourke, one of five prospectors who located a quartz gold lode in 1887. Those five, plus another man, soon located the even more important Iron King and Iron Queen lodes, which were later worked in the Nancy Lee Mine. From three hundred to five hundred rushed to O'Rourke in its first year. But when U.S. Senator Thomas Carter obtained a post office for the village in 1891, Phillip O'Rourke lost the naming honor, and the place became Carter.

In addition to the post office, Carter residents built a butcher shop, a mercantile, Miners' Union Hall, two boarding houses, a hotel, and a school. In two years, though, the Silver Purchase Act's

Left: Keystone.

Below: Pardee before 1896, snugged down amidst the peaks of the Ninemile Divide.
MONTANA HISTORICAL SOCIETY

Above: Keystone, the company town in the Ninemile Divide.
MONTANA HISTORICAL SOCIETY

Left: Keystone's Nancy Lee Mine.

Right: Ore cars from the Haywire Mill.

Below: Keystone.

repeal caused most people to leave.

But there was still gold to be mined, and the town came back beginning in 1904. The following year, Pennsylvania investors bought the Nancy Lee and other mines, and by 1910 Carter had enough people again to apply for a post office. But now there was another settlement named Carter, near Great Falls, so they had to find a different name. Keystone it became—possibly from Pennsylvania's nickname of "Keystone State." The town went on for two more decades until the Nancy Lee was closed. It has been opened from time to time since.

Sylvanite, Keystone

Up on the Yaak River in far northwestern Montana, the Keystone Mine was opened in 1895, after three decades of minimal placer mining. Pete Berg and Bill Lemley had found the first free-milling quartz lode the year before, and the resulting camp combined both names as Lemleyberg. On its platted lots stood a brewery, a sawmill, three stores, a butcher shop, two hotels and two restaurants, and several saloons. Its 500 residents renamed Lemleyberg as Sylvanite, for a type of gold and silver ore.

THE KEYSTONE MINE HAD ITS OWN mill, and then the twenty-stamp Goldflint Mill opened early in 1898. But the free-milling gold broke into complex veins underground, and the mills were closed by August. They stayed closed for a dozen years before a new company of Canadian investors built another mill and a 2,400-foot tramway to deliver Keystone ore to it, and went back to work. That year was 1910, the year of the Great Burn series of vast forest fires in Idaho and western Montana. The mill and mine surface structures, and all but one town building, burned down. The Canadians announced plans to rebuild and even

Above: Core samples from Sylvanite's Haywire Mine.

Right: Haywire Mill, Sylvanite.

A universal problem among upstart mining camps:

Virginia City is ruled by...the hog, which uses the public streets and private gardens according to the demands of its rooting propensities. In other words, it has what may be properly termed the freedom of the city.

(Virginia City)
Montana Post
Oct. 6, 1866

The effect of the city ordinance relating to dogs and hogs has been so beneficial to the community that all parties, excepting those who own swine and wish to feed them at the expense of the public, support these measures. The appearance of the streets has been improved to such an extent that the change is marvellous.

(Virginia City)
Montana Post
Dec. 1, 1866

Left: Near Stark.

Below: Ninemile Community Church in the Ninemile Valley.

ordered lumber, but it didn't come about. A different group of owners opened the mine again from 1931 to 1937.

Montreal, Ninemile, Martina, Stark

Placer mining began on Ninemile Creek in 1874 and claims eventually stretched along sixteen of the creek's eighteen miles and into its feeder gulches and creeks. The gold was very pure, sometimes in nugget form.

The creek's name comes from Nine Mile House, a hotel and stage stop on the Mullan Road nine miles from Frenchtown, right where that military road from Fort Benton to Walla Walla, Washington crossed Ninemile Creek.

Prospectors first used the Ninemile's valley to travel from the Alder Gulch area to strikes in the Kootenay country of British Columbia, and until the mid-1870s didn't slow down long enough to look around. When they did, they found rich placers, the best being on Ninemile Creek itself. Soon thousands of people lived in the complex, and the town of Montreal (also called Old Town) arose at Ninemile Creek's headwaters. Miners could wash up in two

Above: Since the United States didn't fight in the Boer War, Palmer might have been British.

Left: Nature has begun to reclaim dredge tailings piled high on Ninemile Creek near Martina.

Right and below: Since these photos were taken of Stark's last structure, it has been moved to the Ninemile Community Center for reconstruction.

Chinese-owned bathhouses, drink at one of four saloons, and buy supplies from a bakery, a mercantile, and two butcher shops. A town named Martina developed by the San Martina Mine on the valley's northwest side. Most of the area's gold was freighted over the Mullan Road to Lewiston, Idaho, for processing at the Martina City Mill.

By 1879, the easy gold was gone and so were all but about sixty of the prospectors. Chinese workers leased claims and reworked ore dumps, retrieving considerably more gold. Other miners hung on and placered at a low level, keeping certain claims active through the 1920s and 1930s. In 1909, dredging was tried on Kennedy Creek, and Ninemile tributary and, in the 1920s, hydraulicking was attempted on St. Louis Creek. Both times the creeks' sticky blue clay defeated the machines and held its gold. More powerful dredges obtained gold in 1941, and again after the World War II shutdown of nonessential mining.

The Nine Mile and the San Martina mines operated side by side beginning about 1890. Both small mines ran for fifteen years, sending ore down by aerial tramway to a ten-stamp mill in the valley. Besides free-milling gold (at first), the ore carried some silver.

In the lower part of the Ninemile Valley, a lumber mill opened in 1890 to serve the Northern Pacific Railroad. The settlement of Stark developed in between the gold mines and the lumber mill. The Anaconda Copper Mining Company started logging in the area during World War I, but that lasted only ten years, until 1926. Stark itself lingered until the late 1950s.

Above: A stamp-mill drive wheel.

Right: Claim markers at Montreal.

GILT EDGE
KENDALL
MAIDEN
GOLD BUTTE
LANDUSKY
ZORTMAN

NORTH CENTRAL MONTANA

RICH PLACER.

Messrs. Pott & Hayden, have been busily employed… sinking a shaft on their placer claim… After sinking some thirty feet, to bedrock, a drift was run west… but with no paying results. Operations were then inaugurated…east some twenty feet, when, what promises to be a rich deposit, was reached. The owners feel warranted in putting on three shifts, and are confident of striking it immensely rich.

There is no doubt in the minds of practical miners that not only that gulch, but nearly all of this district would prove rich paying placer dig[g]ings, if water could be had in sufficient volume. Messrs. Pott & Hayden are dumping their pay dirt, and with a full flow of water in the spring flood, will wash out the precious metal.

(Maiden)
Mineral Argus
Dec. 20, 1883

Early-day north-central Montana was a lawless place, it seems: settlers grabbed land from Indians, vigilantes chased and hanged stock rustlers in the Missouri Breaks, strangers and even neighbors shot it out in public, shady mine management ripped off hardrock miners—and fired them when they complained! Those "colorful" days may be gone, but some of their wildness is fondly remembered.

JUDITH MOUNTAINS

Maiden, Gilt Edge

Placer gold prospectors didn't make it into the Judith Mountains until after many of western Montana's gold camps had faded away. Placer gold was found by a party moving west into this country from the Black Hills in 1880, but lack of water was a problem for placering.

That June, lode gold was struck in four locations, including what was later named Maiden Gulch. The following year, C. C. Snow and J. R. Kemper, two of the discoverers, set up the townsite of

Above: Maiden in 1888; Bellanger's Store is the large white building in the center.
MONTANA HISTORICAL SOCIETY

Below: Maiden today.

*Right and below: Maiden—
still home to a very few.*

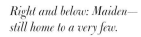

Above: Bellanger's Store, Maiden.

*Right: The Whitney bull train
at Maiden in 1882.*

MONTANA HISTORICAL SOCIETY

Maiden by building fences around the lots rather than platting it on a map. Since these lots were on land belonging to Fort Maginnis, they were challenging the U.S. Army. At her mother's suggestion, they named the settlement after the daughter of friends, a girl they had been calling "Little Maiden."

In a year's time, Maiden was a substantial settlement serving residents and miners from the surrounding gulches. It boasted both a doctor and an attorney— S. C. Edgerton, in fact, son of the Sidney Edgerton who had lived in Bannack and helped create Montana Territory, then

was appointed its first governor. People living in log or frame homes could choose between two clothing stores and among six mercantiles; services included an assayer and an Omaha firm's ore-buyer, two barbers, a blacksmith and a stable, a hotel and a restaurant and, of course, eight saloons. By 1885, now with thirteen saloons and heading for its 1888 peak population of 1,200, the town spread along three streets.

The army made its move on the two-year-old town in 1883 by posting flyers announcing that Fort Maginnis land had to be vacated by civilians within sixty

Maude Morton (later Nylander), just out of teacher's college, arrived to teach third and fourth grade in Kendall in 1910. She boarded with Mr. and Mrs. Tom Matlock, owners of the mercantile. She recalled:

The Matlock home joined the store, and right across the street was the Rock Saloon. The sheepherders and cowboys would come in there to celebrate when they drew their paychecks. Many times they would go outside and shoot into the air and yell, and I would crawl down into my big feather bed, cover my head and pray that a stray bullet would not come our way.

Lewistown Daily News
June 10, 1962

Every birth in Maiden excepting one, has been a girl. Maiden is non-productive of males. Instinctively she seems to know the most pressing needs of Montana.

(Lewistown)
Mineral Argus
August 7, 1884

DEVELOP YOUR LEADS.

If we are going to have a lively camp next summer some hard work needs to be done this winter.... Every man that has a claim, should make an effort to "show up" something. Capitalists are not buying holes in the ground. They want to see something on the dump. If you havn't got any thing of value, throw it up and go to driving bull teams, or engage in some other remunerative labor. There are a certain class of men who find the summer "too warm" and the winter "too cold" to work, consequently they are always dead broke. They seem to be waiting for the melenium or something else to take them by the boot straps and raise them up from poverty to wealth, instantaneously.

(Maiden)
Mineral Argus
Dec. 27, 1883

Left: Gilt Edge.
MONTANA HISTORICAL SOCIETY

Below: Lilacs continue to bloom by the Gilt Edge schoolhouse.

Center: Gilt Edge.

days. After residents presented petitions on behalf of Maiden's existence, the army blinked, and moved its border away from the townsite.

Maiden even tried to become the seat of Fergus County, but it lost to Lewistown. When the mines began to fail, that sealed Maiden's fate. Only 200 souls called it home by 1896, and nine years later the town didn't rebuild after fire swept through.

PLACERING BEGAN IN GILT EDGE IN 1880, and lode mining the following year, but the town didn't come along until

August 1893, when a group of Great Falls investors put in a $35,000 cyanide plant at the Gilt Edge Mine. But things got off to a wobbly business start. By the time a brutal winter set in, and while false-front business buildings were under construction, the owners began missing paydays. When half the fifty workers complained to manager H. S. Sherard, they got their back pay—along with their walking papers. The others got worthless checks that they spent in Lewistown. Now those merchants were entangled in the fray. Robert A. Ammon, a new manager, heard that the county sheriff was

Above: Hoist wheel, Gilt Edge.

Left: Cyanide vat, Gilt Edge.

Right: Kendall in 1911, as viewed from near the Barnes-King Mine adit. Numerals indicate: 1. Miner's Union Hospital; 2. Miners Union Hall; 3. Jones Opera House; 4. First State Bank of Kendall; 5. Shaules Hotel; 6. Wedge Buffet (saloon); 7. Nathan Butler Dry Goods; 8. Matlock's General Store; 9. Kendall Hotel.
MONTANA HISTORICAL SOCIETY

Below: A comfortable Gilt Edge home.

Bottom: Tailings pile from the Gilt Edge Mill.

Right: Evidence of drilling contests remains at Kendall.

Far right: Solomon Koko on his way to winning first place in the single-jack drilling contest on Miners' Union Day, June 13, 1910, at Kendall.
MONTANA HISTORICAL SOCIETY

coming to seize the property. Chased by the sheriff, he took the gold bullion on hand and headed for Great Falls, sold it to a bank, and paid off a major creditor.

When the sheriff closed the mine and mill, he distributed supplies found warehoused there, while Lewistown housewives sent two wagons full of food to save Gilt Edge families.

That was the first six months!

Gilt Edge had largely been abandoned by the time a new corporation took over the mine in 1897. The next year, the mine was back in production, and the following year a new mill was erected.

Population was up to 350 in 1900, and in 1907 the mine ran three shifts and the town housed 1,500 people. But the ore thinned out and the mine closed in 1909. Later reworking of tailings didn't bring the town back to life.

NORTH MOCCASIN MOUNTAINS

Kendall

In the late 1890s, several combined lode and open-pit mines opened in the

Dave Jones ran "a number of tons of Spotted Horse ore through the Davis arrastre [*sic*]," which "proved a greater success than was anticipated…considering the imperfection of the machinery, the unavoidable waste, and the great cost of taking out and reducing the ore…[which] can only be accounted for by the ore being much richer than expected, and if reduced by modern means and clean-up would have been much greater and the expense less.

Twenty-three tons of ore was mined and run through the arrastre; necessitating the labor of two miners and two men at the arrastre and a team to haul the ore from mine to mill, involving an outlay of $337.50. From this ore forty-three and one-half ounces of bullion was cleaned up, which, at the value…of $18 per ounce, gives a total valuation of $787; leaving $450.50 over cost of mining and reducing.

By these figures it will be seen the ore averaged a little over $34.20. With this result from an old time Mexican arrastre, it is but reasonable to estimate that with modern machinery, the ore would run…$50.00 to the ton.

(Lewistown)
Mineral Argus
June 26, 1884

North Moccasin Mountains, putting out ore worth only $5 to $9 in gold per ton. The new cyanide process was just what this ore needed, and when Harry T. Kendall put in such a mill in 1900, the area's boom was on.

The next year, homesteader William A. Shaules platted a townsite, named Kendall, on his property and sold lots. By October, two coaches full of ladies of the evening had staffed one of the new buildings, but there were also the wedge-shaped Shaules Hotel at a three-way intersection, a bank, a newspaper, Miners' Union and fraternal halls,

saloons, restaurants, and stores. All the buildings received electricity from the water plant. Shortly, two stage-coaches a day connected with Lewistown, an automobile soon offered freight delivery to and from the county seat, and rumors circulated about a railroad spur. The Jones Opera House and a Presbyterian church would be built by 1907.

Fifteen hundred people lived here until one of the four main mines closed in 1920 and the end began. In the 1930s, a small amount of placer activity cleaned up what little loose gold there was.

Left: Kendall foundation.

Below: Double-jack drilling took great trust, as seen here in the 1910 Miners' Union Day contest at Kendall. This team is Jack Drinville and son James.
MONTANA HISTORICAL SOCIETY

Above: At the Kendall Gold Mine's 600-foot level in 1909, a miner works with a single-jack compressed air drill, commonly called a "bumble bee." His candle holder is stuck into a supporting timber.
MONTANA HISTORICAL SOCIETY

Left: First Presbyterian Church, Kendall.

STUART'S STRANGLERS

Granville Stuart had been in Alder Gulch, on the right side of the law, where he was part of the early 1860s Vigilante activity.

Two decades later, he was the managing partner of the DHS Ranch near Fort Maginnis in central Montana, with two others who had made more money in mining and other enterprises than hard-luck Granville did: A. J. Davis and Samuel T. Hauser. Stuart set up the ranch in 1880, and had witnessed the boom in stock rustling at the DHS southeast of the Judith Mountains—and all around the area. Rustlers rounded up cattle, sheep, and horses, and used the rough Missouri Breaks country to herd the animals to Canada or Dakota Territory.

Serving in the 1883 territorial legislature's upper house, Stuart had carried a bill that stockmen supported, to create a Board of Stock Commissioners empowered to arrest suspected rustlers. Governor John Schuyler Crosby vetoed the bill because it drew from general tax monies to benefit a single field of business, and he thought it granted the board too much police power.

In spring of the following year, Montana Stock Growers Association met in Miles City and strongly debated what to do with the rustlers. Members Theodore Roosevelt and the Marquis de Mores, who ranched in Dakota, agreed with those who wanted to create a "cowboy army" and ride out at once. Cooler heads prevailed, at least in terms of public statements. The association made no official plans to deal with rustlers.

But stockmen organized in the old way, the vigilante way Stuart (and surely others who'd passed through Alder Gulch) knew well.

Then came the Fourth of July, and two widely suspected rustler bosses—in all their arrogance—had a fine time getting drunk in Lewistown. Rattlesnake Jake (Charles Fallon) and Longhair (Edward Owen) beat up a citizen before starting to shoot up the town.

To the bad guys' amazement, the citizens didn't step aside as usual, but stepped into sight, well armed, in doorways all along Lewistown's business street. They killed Rattlesnake Jake with nine bullet hits and Longhair with eleven, thus declaring war on rustlers.

The central Montana vigilantes rode far and wide, from the Musselshell to the upper Yellowstone River, and hanged at least fifteen, and as many as sixty rustlers. They were soon nicknamed Stuart's Stranglers—not that Granville said he had anything to do with them—and their story played out that summer:

The little affair at Lewistown is very liable to be duplicated at Maiden most any time. Citizens who have revolvers or Winchesters should keep a supply of ammunition on hand and weapons loaded, in case they should be called on suddenly. Outlaws may attempt to "paint our town red" some day, in such case we should be prepared to give them a warm reception.

(Maiden) *Mineral Argus*, July 10, 1884

Granville Stuart

The people...seem determined to make it exceedingly sultry for horse thieves from this time forward. Great care should be used however, in dealing with this evil. No innocent man should be made to suffer on suspicion or circumstantial evidence. Positive proof should be the only condition under which rash measures are adopted.

(Maiden) *Mineral Argus*, July 11, 1884

We learn from reliable sources that "Dutch Louis"...was hung last week by a party of men, on the c[h]arge of keeping a rendezvous for horse thieves [at his ranch]. It is said he bore a hard name and suspicion has been resting on him for some time. We are unable to learn particulars.

(Maiden) *Mineral Argus*, July 24, 1884

A telegram dated July 23d, from Captain of the steamer Benton [traveling on the Missouri River], was received at Ft. Maginnis, stating that the bodies of seven men were seen hanging to trees at the mouth of the Musselshell [River].

(Maiden) *Mineral Argus*, July 24, 1884

The report in regard to the hanging of "Dutch Louie" is pronounced false.

(Maiden) *Mineral Argus*, July 31, 1884

The papers are full of stories about the hanging of horse thieves in Eastern Meagher county, but find it difficult to ascertain the facts in regard to really how many have been killed and hung. From the best information only about seventeen have shared this fate from first to last; yet, from the rumors afloat one would think that not less than fifty had come to their end at the hand of exasperated cowboys.

Rocky Mountain Husbandman, quoted in (Maiden) *Mineral Argus*, Aug. 21, 1884

Granville Stuart informed us that sixty-nine head of horses recovered from the horse thieves, are held at his ranch, awaiting identification.

(Maiden) *Mineral Argus*, Aug. 28, 1884

Beginning in the September 4, 1884, issue of the *Mineral Argus*, Stuart, Kohrs & Company ran an ad describing the captured horses being kept for claiming at their Fort Maginnis–area ranch.

Hon. James Fergus [Republican legislator] tells a... reporter that he has been instrumental in getting Granville Stuart to kill [D]emocrats for horse theives, and when Granville realized the extent of the trick he became sick. Mr. Fergus thinks his chances for the legislature are much enhanced by the killings. If Fergus is thus affected by Helena atmosphere, he had better return to his ranch.

(Maiden) *Mineral Argus*, Sept. 18, 1884

LITTLE ROCKY MOUNTAINS

Landusky, Zortman

Taller than most men, Powell Landusky also had a powerful temper, was an excellent shot, and seemed not to know fear. It was said he never killed a white man, just beat them up badly. He worked hard on Montana's gold frontier, but on both sides of the law. He hated Indians but was willing to take their money for whisky. He was generous to his friends and raised a family of stepchildren on his ranch. After a Blackfeet shot off part of his jaw, he must have been as fearsome to look at as he was fearsome acting when riled.

Powell was only fourteen in 1864 when he left his home north of St. Louis, Missouri, and took a steamboat up the Missouri River to Fort Benton. In Last Chance Gulch (Helena) that year, another man asked teasingly where he might be from with that accent. After punching and cursing the fellow, Landusky answered, "Pike County, Missouri," and he was called Pike ever after.

Pike left Last Chance in four years, and until 1880 worked as a trapper and a woodhawk (chopping wood and leaving it along the Missouri for steamboats to pick up) in central Montana. In 1880, having partnered with two men to open a trading post, a drunken Pike fired his rifle into a Blackfeet lodge and killed a woman. Another Blackfeet fired at Landusky, hitting his jaw. Landusky pulled out a segment of jaw that held four teeth and threw it on the ground, ready to fight some more until his partners stepped in. During the week it took them to get Landusky to a Lewistown doctor, and the week and a half after-

Right: Turn-of-the-20th-century Landusky.
MONTANA HISTORICAL SOCIETY

Below: The Kendall stage has a full load one day in 1903.
MONTANA HISTORICAL SOCIETY

Above: Honest advertising at a Kendall Miners' Union Day picnic.
MONTANA HISTORICAL SOCIETY

Right: Landusky.

ward, the wounded man stayed drunk.

The next year, he and one of those partners opened a saloon in Maiden. His wedding to the widow Dessery, the mother of "several children," is thought to have been the town's first marriage ceremony. In 1884, he took the family to live on a ranch in what was called Little Alder Gulch in the Little Rocky Mountains. He was among men who found placer gold there that same year, but the gold didn't last long and Landusky was riding the range for Granville Stuart and the Pioneer Cattle Company a couple years later—just in time to experience the "hard winter of 1886–1887." A drought year followed by horrendous winter weather beginning late in 1886 marked the end of Montana's open-range cattle industry when thousands of cattle died off.

In 1890, Landusky located two gold lodes in the Little Rockies: the Julia and the Gold Bug. He did well working them alone, also working as a building constructor and serving as a deputy sheriff.

Alongside one of his mining claims, and also on a ranch near his, lived the Logan brothers: Harvey, John, and Lonnie. Harvey sometimes went by the name

Left: Landusky miners relax outside their cabin, circa 1896.
MONTANA HISTORICAL SOCIETY

Below: Mixed building styles at Zortman.

Mining engineer Henry Parrent arrived in Gilt Edge in 1898 to build a mill for L. G. Phelps and E. W. King, and later had this tale to tell about a famous resident:

I was sitting in a poker game one night and a tin horn gambler was taking my money away from me right and left. I didn't have sense enough to realize that the game was crooked until I had lost nearly everything I had and was pushing my chair back to leave.

A deep bass voice spoke from behind me; "stay right where you are, young fellow. I'll see that you get fair play."

It was Calamity Jane and she had a nice little gun poking right into the middle of our card game. Well I stayed where I was and somehow or other, my luck began to change and I came out the winner by a whole lot. I can thank Calamity Jane for that.

Great Falls Tribune
Nov. 22, 1936

of "Kid Curry," and the trio were the core of the Curry Gang of rustlers and robbers. Landusky got along fine with the outlaws until 1892, when Lonnie got interested in one of Pike's stepdaughters and Pike did not approve. A feud was on, with area residents taking sides.

When the Curry Gang was caught altering brands, Deputy Landusky escorted Harvey and John Logan to jail in Fort Benton. There, rumor had it, he chained them to the wall and beat them up. The rustlers said he had trumped up the charges to try to get their mining claims and ranch. The feud continued.

In 1893, Pike and his son-in-law (a young man Pike obviously did approve of) stumbled onto another gold lode. Landusky himself staked thirty more claims in the area as prospectors rushed in. In 1894, residents named their settlement Landusky. It soon was known for its violence, and the story was that no natural deaths occurred for fourteen years. There also was enough feeling of community that a town meeting voted to hold a big Christmas feast and dance in 1894. John Logan volunteered his barn, Lonnie put together a dance band with himself as fiddler and

Above: A quiet day in Gilt Edge, circa 1897, leads Calamity Jane (Martha Jane Canary) and cowboy E.C. "Teddy Blue" Abbott outdoors to toast the camera and model each other's hats.
MONTANA HISTORICAL SOCIETY

Left: Zortman neighborhood.

Right: Rooms without a view.

Below: One-time store on Zortman's main street.

Above: Zortman cemetery.

Right: Zortman townsite.
MONTANA HISTORICAL SOCIETY

leader, and sent a wagon to a nearby ranch to borrow an organ.

The party lasted for two days and drew in a hundred area men of varying degrees of lawfulness who joined Landusky residents. But peace reigned until festivities ended on December 26.

The following morning, Pike went into Jake's Saloon and found Lonnie Logan already there. Then Harvey came in and punched and knocked down Pike, who was fifty-four years old and wrapped in a stiff buffalo coat against the extreme cold. Logan continued punching Pike's face and banging his head against the floor while everyone else refused to intervene. Still, Landusky was able to get up, draw his gun, and pull the trigger before Harvey got to his. Landusky's gun misfired, and Kid Curry shot Pike twice, fatally, before he, Lonnie, and another gang member escaped.

Pike's family went on running the Gold Bug Mine until they sold it in 1902. The mine was opened off and on into the 1960s.

The town of Landusky faded until the cyanide process came along, and prosperity returned from 1903 to 1912. After President Franklin Roosevelt raised the

Rough frontier and modern town culture existed side-by-side in Montana's later mining camps, as these items a week apart in the Maiden newspaper show.

Did anyone see who was doing the great "pistol practice act" Sunday night? If so, the best thing he can do, as a citizen desiring to see the laws of the territory effective instead of a farce, is to make complaint before a justice of the piece [sic] who will give him the full extent of the law.

(Maiden)
Mineral Argus
May 22, 1884

The Maiden base-ball club is making rapid improvement in their playing.

(Maiden)
Mineral Argus
May 29, 1884

Left: Gold Butte.
MONTANA HISTORICAL SOCIETY

Below: A Gold Butte adit.

price of gold during the Depression, 1934 saw better times once again. Wildfire in July 1936 came to the edge of town as it burned across 23,000 acres. Only two days after that, a fire began in a Landusky mill and burned toward Zortman. Area miners, ranchers, Fort Belknap Indian Reservation firefighters, Civilian Conservation Corps, and Forest Service workers fought both blazes.

Zortman

Indians who knew of gold in the Zortman area tried to keep it a secret, to prevent a rush of whites; white prospectors in the late 1860s checked out the area and gave up on it. When Pete Zortman located the Alabama Mine in 1899, his own and others' prosperity began. Cyanide processing was necessary for this ore, which was mined off and on into the 1920s. The Depression-era raising of gold prices encouraged another spurt of mining, which lasted until World War II shut down production, picked up after the war and ended again in 1951. Many of Zortman's buildings burned down in major fires, the first in 1929 and the second in 1944.

In 1979, the world's first cyanide heap-leach open-pit mine was opened at Zortman by Pegasus Gold Corporation. This process could retrieve gold from amazingly weak ores. Pegasus employed as many as 225 people here until it shut the mine and declared bankruptcy late in the 1990s. In 1998, the federal Bureau of Land Management and Montana Department of Environmental Quality began overseeing site cleanup after Pegasus forfeited reclamation bonds in the amount of $30 million.

Gold Butte

In 1885, prospectors starting their first full season exploring the Sweet Grass Hills hadn't bothered to find out they were on land that was then part of the Blackfeet Indian Reservation. When word got to Washington, D.C., that year, the Commissioner of Indian Affairs told the Blackfeet's agent to evict the miners. Instead, somehow an infantry company was sent to settle in near the camp of Gold Butte, apparently protecting miners who dug in land sacred to the Blackfeet. Gold mining finally ceased around 1890.

Above: Settling pond, Gold Butte.

GLOSSARY

Adit—Horizontal mine entrance, into the side of a hill, as opposed to "shaft."

Amalgamation—Uses the chemical reaction between silver or gold with mercury to extract the precious metal from ore; part of the milling process. The mercury, which ignites at a lower temperature than paper, is then burned off.

Arrastra—The simplest form of rock-crushing equipment, which could be built and run with little investment. A horse (sometimes even a miner) attached to a center pole walked in a circle dragging a heavy object over ore spread on the ground. The crushed rock was sorted into waste and "colors." Arrastras worked best with free-milling gold.

Assay—To measure the proportion of valuable minerals to waste rock in an ore sample.

Bullion—Nearly pure gold or silver shaped into ingots or bars for transport and sale.

Claim—Legal description of the surface area a miner is working, or the surface area from which an underground mine descends.

Concentration mill or **concentrator**—General term covering mills that crush and sort but do not smelt ore.

Cyanide process—A form of leaching minerals from ore that was invented late in the 19th century, and continued to be refined to process more and more complex (less concentrated) ores.

Dredges—See Placer mining.

Float or **free gold**—See Placer deposits.

Free-milling gold—Gold that is so well concentrated in its ore that most of the gold can be retrieved by milling alone. "Complex" gold ore has smaller, more fractured veins, and requires smelting after milling.

Hard-rock mining—See Lode mining.

Head buildings—Surface structures above a mine shaft, including those housing the cable apparatus that operated elevators for men and ore. "Head frame" or "gallows frame" is the structure that operates the cables.

Hydraulic mining—See Placer mining.

Leaching—Using water or acid to remove waste ore, in a tank or other large contained space. See also Cyanide process.

Lode mining—Underground mining that includes setting explosives and using jackhammers to tear through hard rock in following veins (deposits) of ore. In both shallow and deep mines, sturdy timbers had to be set in place to support rock surrounding the opening where miners worked.

Mill—Where ore is crushed and metal-bearing rock sorted from waste rock. Montana mills most often were built on hillsides so that gravity pulled ore down chutes from one process to the next. A mill's product is concentrated ore, which goes to a smelter for refining.

Ball mill employs round weights in a large drum to crush ore poured into it.

Stamp mill crushes ore under vertically-dropped, powered, metal stamps.

Placer deposits—Pieces of gold (from sand-sized "dust" to "flakes" and larger "nuggets") that weather has eroded from rock, and water has carried downstream.

Placer mining—Using water to wash heavy minerals (including free or float gold) out of sand and/or gravel. In order of complexity:

Panning uses a hand-held, wide, flat, metal pan, with water gently rolled around in it to carry away dirt and let gold nuggets sink to the bottom.

Sluicing uses the same washing idea, but with a rocking or angled "cradle" (often made of wood) that holds a large quantity of dirt; water is gravity-fed through flood gates, and gold catches on "riffles," crosswise wooden slats.

Dredges are floating platforms that move through shallow water and scoop dirt and gravel that passes through a washing process; waste dirt and stone pile up behind as "tailings."

Hydraulic mining takes the washing principle to its ultimate: high-pressure water hoses tear down an entire hillside and wash the ore.

Quartz lode or **quartz mining**—See Lode mining.

Shaft—A vertical mine entrance, dug down into bedrock, as opposed to "adit."

Smelter—Uses heat to extract nearly pure metals from concentrated ore.

Tailings—Waste rock left after ore is processed. Along streams that were dredged, tailings piles are conical mounds of sand and gravel; around smelters they are shiny slag heaps.

Waste dump—Stores rock removed from an underground mine as shafts and tunnels are dug.

INDEX

1881 map of Montana post office towns and railroad stations.

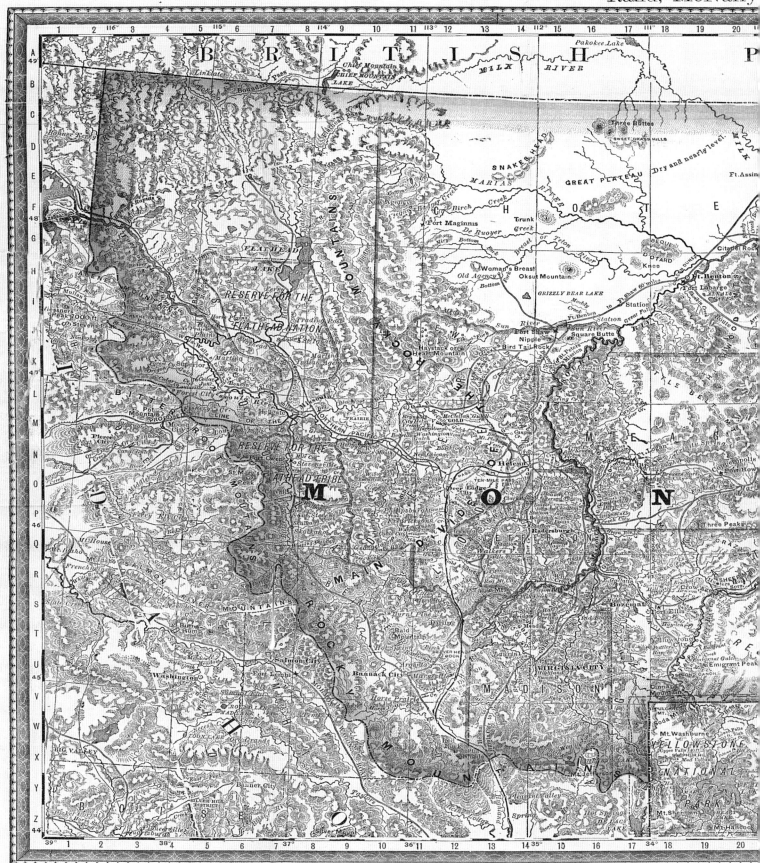

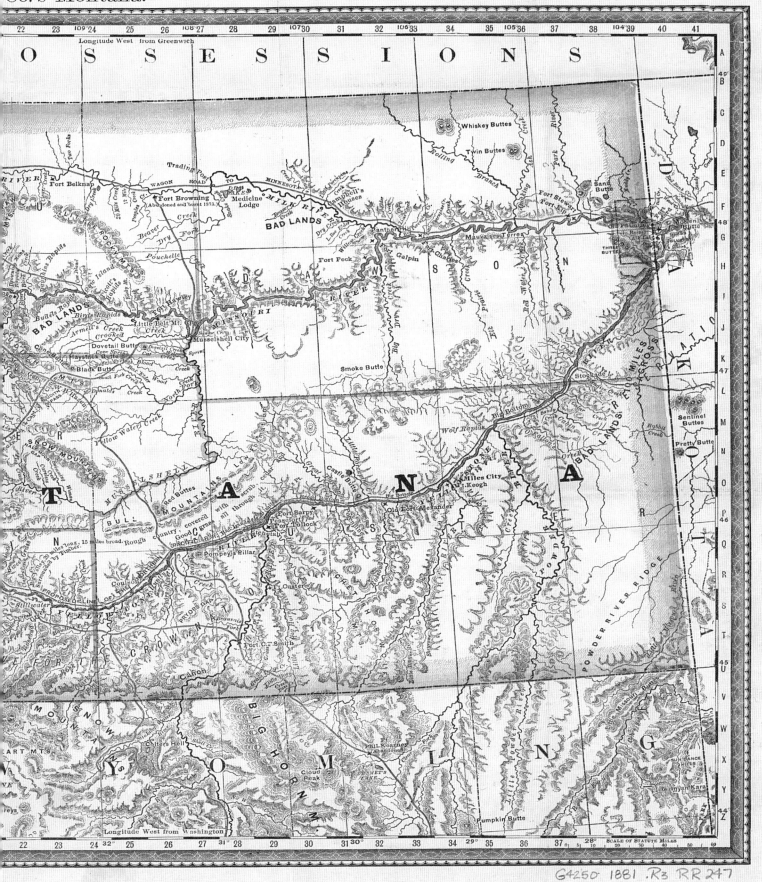

Panning and sluicing in Alder Gulch, around 1870.